JASMIR CREED
DYSTOPOLIS

Victoria Gallery and Museum,
University of Liverpool

Exhibition of Paintings

16 November 2018 – 20 April 2019

Edited by Jasmir Creed and Jai Chuhan
www.jcreed1.wixsite.com/creart
www.jchuhan333.wixsite.com/paintings

Published in 2018 by Victoria Gallery and Museum, University of Liverpool.
www.vgm.liv.ac.uk

Design by Mike Carney

Distributed worldwide by Liverpool University Press
4 Cambridge Street, Liverpool L69 7ZU United Kingdom.

ISBN 978-0-9563595-2-0

A CIP catalogue record of this book is available from the British Library.

Acknowledgements and grateful thanks to: The team at Victoria Gallery
and Museum especially Amanda Draper, Curator of Exhibitions (Art);
Alnoor Mitha, Artistic Director of Asia Triennial Manchester and Senior
Research Fellow at Manchester Metropolitan University; Dr. Graeme
Gilloch, Sociologist Lecturer at Lancaster University; Dr Lauren Elkin,
Lecturer in English, University of Liverpool, Jai Chuhan, artist and
Professor at LJMU Liverpool School of Art & Design.

Supported by Victoria Gallery and Museum, University of Liverpool
and Liverpool University Press

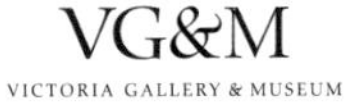
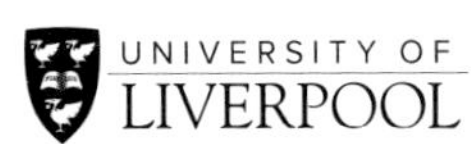
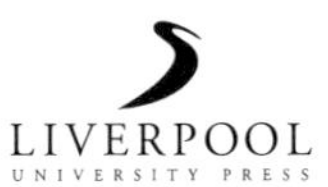
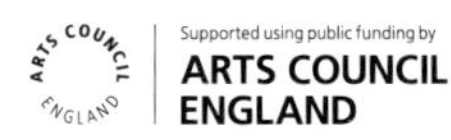
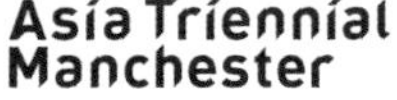

CONTENTS

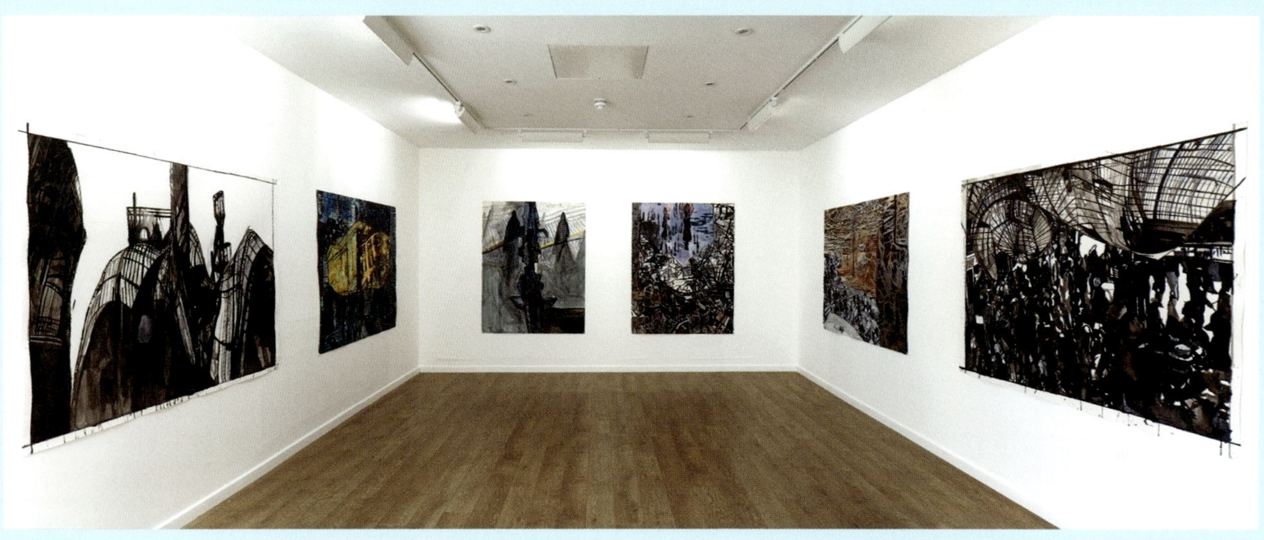

Urban Forest, solo exhibition at Delta House Studios, London 2017

FOREWORD
AMANDA DRAPER

Jasmir Creed first met the VGM team when she attended a study day here held by the Contemporary Art Society. She was a quiet but deeply focussed and intellectual presence. During a break, Jasmir was persuaded to show some images of her work on her phone. We were intrigued. *Dystopolis* is the culmination of that day in February 2018.

What immediately appealed about Jasmir's work was her dynamic mark-making and the thoughtful story-telling instilled in each painting. A city-dweller all her life, Jasmir embodies in her art the dualism experienced in the urban environment. On the one hand, there is exhilaration at being part of a crowd and exploring an ever changing landscape. But on the other hand, this constant over-writing of a familiar internalised map with new skyscrapers and transport infrastructures, along with the potential for attack we all currently live with, can give an unsettling undercurrent.

To create her work Jasmir immerses herself in the cityscape. This can be London, her home town of Manchester and neighbouring Salford or, more recently, Liverpool. She sees herself as a *flâneuse*, the female equivalent of the men who strolled around late 19th century Paris blending in with the crowds and yet observing others, as defined by Charles Baudelaire. Rather than popular landmarks, Jasmir is drawn to places of transit such as railway stations or those small, unexpected spaces of city greenery. Places where people might stop for a short while before getting on with their lives. She ponders about these lives and how she is perceived by these passers-by, if at all.

INEFFABLE CITY
LAUREN ELKIN

Translation is always a form of distortion, and what we see, looking at one of Jasmir Creed's canvases, is a kind of translation, of the city rendered through the artist's perceptive gaze, and her creative body. Creed's city will not be your city, or my city, but a very personal one, whose architecture and graffiti and swells of people register on the canvas in her own unique visual patois.

Working mostly from photographs, and in part from her walks through cities like London, Manchester, and now Liverpool, Creed is attuned to the surrealist juxtapositions the city throws in our paths – much like the painter Dexter Dalwood, whose hyperreal interiors are a clear influence here. She lives and works amidst the neoclassical, industrial cityscape of Manchester, where she finds herself enjoyably lost in the crowd, left alone to attune herself to the noises of the city, or to the soundtrack on her headphones as she walks. What might the people around her be thinking as she passes them? How does this generate a psychic charge to a given street? Creed is aiming for fidelity to that psychogeography, while creating her own visual world that owes no debt of representation to the original.

I love the way her work kettles the crowd in the geometry of the city, as in *Whirlpool*, or in the radiant impasto of *Naturopen*, which situates a drab, colourless group of people crowded into a bland beige space covered over or interrupted by a bright lily pond which has about it the keen artificiality of mall horticulture. Is this Liverpool One, a place where you can walk for hours without seeing the sky, or without knowing for sure if what is above your head is sky, sky perceived through window, or ceiling made to look like sky? Or some ineffable city, a translation of our own, one we need Creed to make visible to us? Creed picks up on the urban paradoxes of Liverpool and allows the viewer to enter them herself, in a gesture that both distorts and makes legible the habitats that we urgently need to see afresh, if we are to understand ourselves at all.

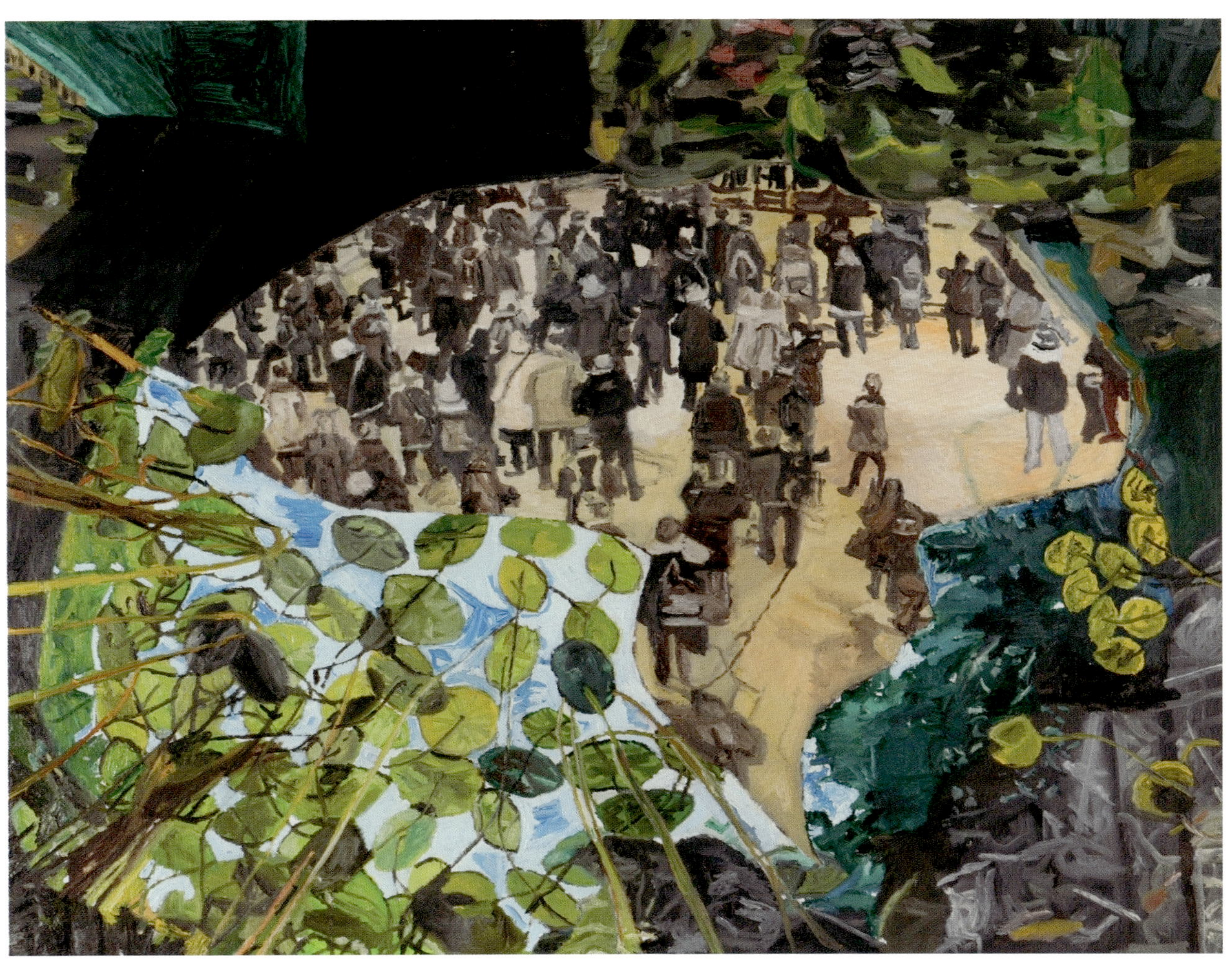

NATUROPEN 2017
Oil on canvas 120 x 90 cm

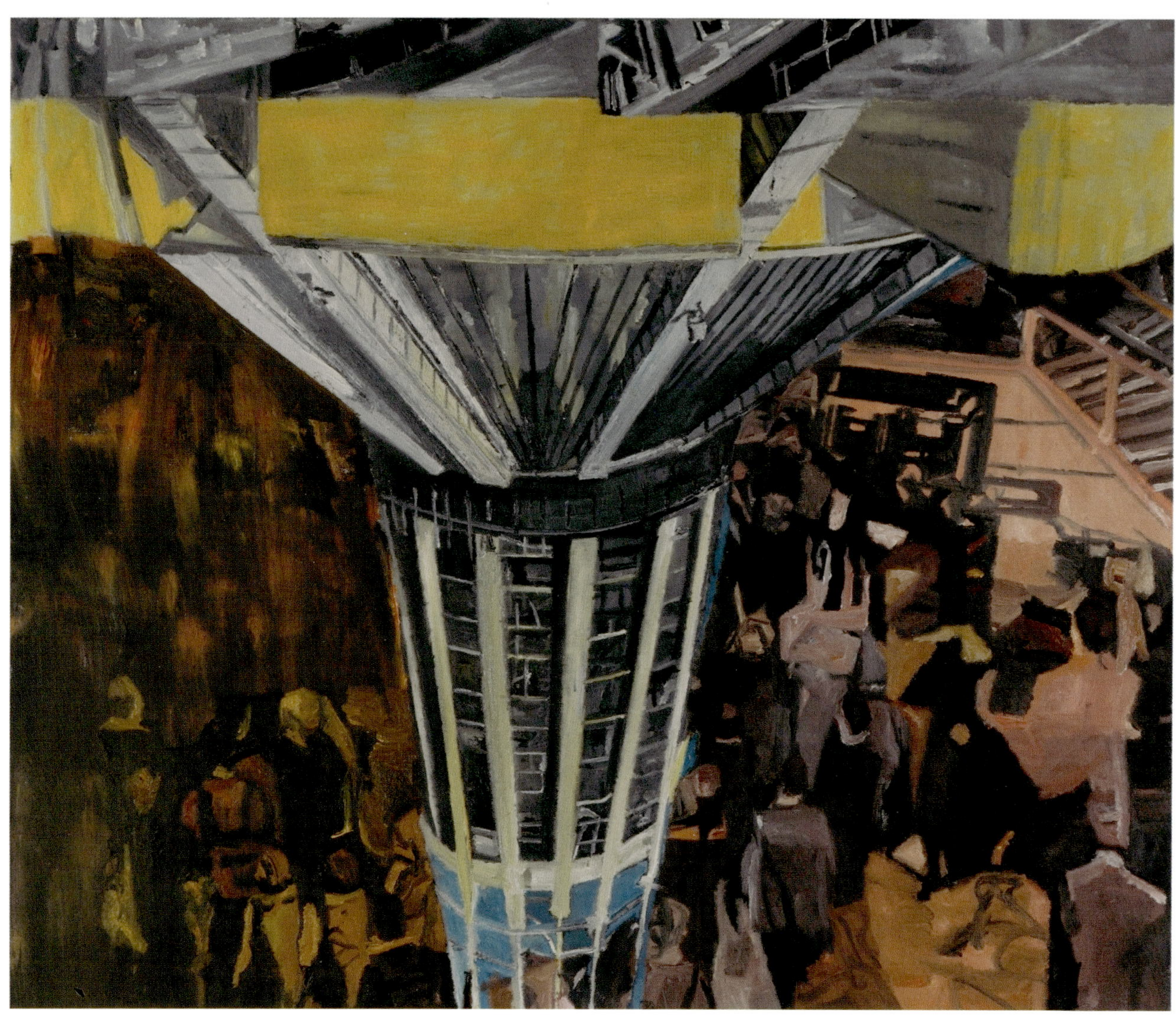

SOMETIMES LOST 2018
Oil on canvas 120 x 90 cm

DYSTOPOLIS
JASMIR CREED

I am exploring the possibilities for the painted narrative based on personal psycho-geographic journeys through city environments. My paintings explore the cultivation of spaces, physical and otherwise e.g. virtual, in cities including Manchester and London, focussing on architecture and crowds. Multiple viewpoints express feelings of alienation and flux in the jostling movement of people in urban spaces, showing the city as a dense environment for the familiar and unfamiliar. I consider how views of contemporary urban journeys and the structure of crowds, the shape and nature of crowds such as commuters, political marches, translate into contemporary painting.

On my journeys through cities I observe crowds in flux in spaces of temporary transit such as railway stations and streets. Organic crowd forms flit in and out of each other juxtaposed with man-made architecture. I am fascinated by iconic buildings such as Imperial War Museum North designed by Daniel Liebskind. I notice there the slow movement of visitors such as families and war veterans reacting to images of crowds in the exhibits e.g. soldiers in conflict. I paint and draw the architecture as if it is closing in on the viewer, accentuated by monochromatic colour combinations, with the shape of crowds indicating its nature e.g. as a swarm unwelcomed by some, mechanistic commuters, random walkers or orchestrated as in political marches or memorial parades.

I am interested in how people experience the city in the contemporary digital age. Charles Baudelaire identified the flâneur as a stroller and observer in his essay *The Painter of Modern Life* (1863). The flâneur and urban explorer in the 19th century was usually a wealthy man of leisure whereas I am a female urban wanderer, honing my images to reflect my responses to contemporary cities, engaging physically to locations, and also to my journeys in digital illusionary spaces. Marc Auge in *Non-Places – Introduction to an Anthropology of Supermodernity* (1992) discusses excess and over-abundance of time, ego and space e.g. virtual, being overloaded and constantly bombarded with information. I find it interesting that in virtual platforms users navigate virtual space and interact as if in the physical world, socializing and creating little virtual worlds even if some appear like fantasy worlds.

The use of chance in my work is an important factor in its production, based on experimentation with montage using photographs of different environments that I take. My montages are hand made with printed material rather than using digital processes, and create surrealistic juxtapositions forming visual dialogues to create a sense of strangeness about otherwise familiar everyday scenes. The use of physical materials enables processing of multiple images into a personal distillation. Franz Ackermann's paintings and painted wall installations focus on themes of global tourism and urbanism considering non-places including underpasses. My work does this but in a different painterly language. Non-place environments are present in Edward Hopper's paintings e.g. *Approaching the City* (1946) that shows an underpass with railway tracks and an unseen traveller neither completely in the city or outside of it, similarly to the sense of flux in my paintings e.g. *Sometimes Lost* (2018).

In my paintings of modern life of today I voyeuristically observe figures in spaces concerned with the uncanny experience of the modern metropolitan environment. Peter Ackroyd's book *London* describes the city metaphorically as a biography of a person constantly evolving similarly to my use of autobiographical responses to urban environments.

The artist Julie Mehretu explores abstracted images of cities, histories, wars and geographies with a frenetic mark making that for the artist becomes a way of unravelling a personal biography similar to my use of topological maps in my painting. Andreas Gursky's photographs of crowds including of Tokyo Stock exchange show an aerial view similarly to the viewpoint in my painting *Fragmentation* (2017). Kathy Prenderghast's map drawings psycho-geographically show capital cities. Her network of lines convey patterns of routes through each city. I use aerial viewpoints of maps for the purposes of symbolizing routes I take as a flâneur around urban environments, strolling and responding to man-made forms and viewpoints e.g. my painting *Aerial Space* (2016).

My images show the city as a rich forest-like environment of the known and the unknown. The unsettling architecture that I see is domineering, creating a dystopic sense of a metropolis, illustrating an atmosphere of alienation in the urban environment, as an individual confronting crowds weaving through cities.

NOTES
Ackroyd, P. (2000) *London the Biography*, London: Chatto and Windus
Auge, M. (2008) *Non-places: an introduction to Supermodernity*, 2nd ed. London: Verso
Baudelaire, C. (1995) *The Painter of Modern Life and Other Essays (Arts and Letters)*, Phaidon Press
Solinit, R. (2014) *Wanderlust a History of Walking*, Granta

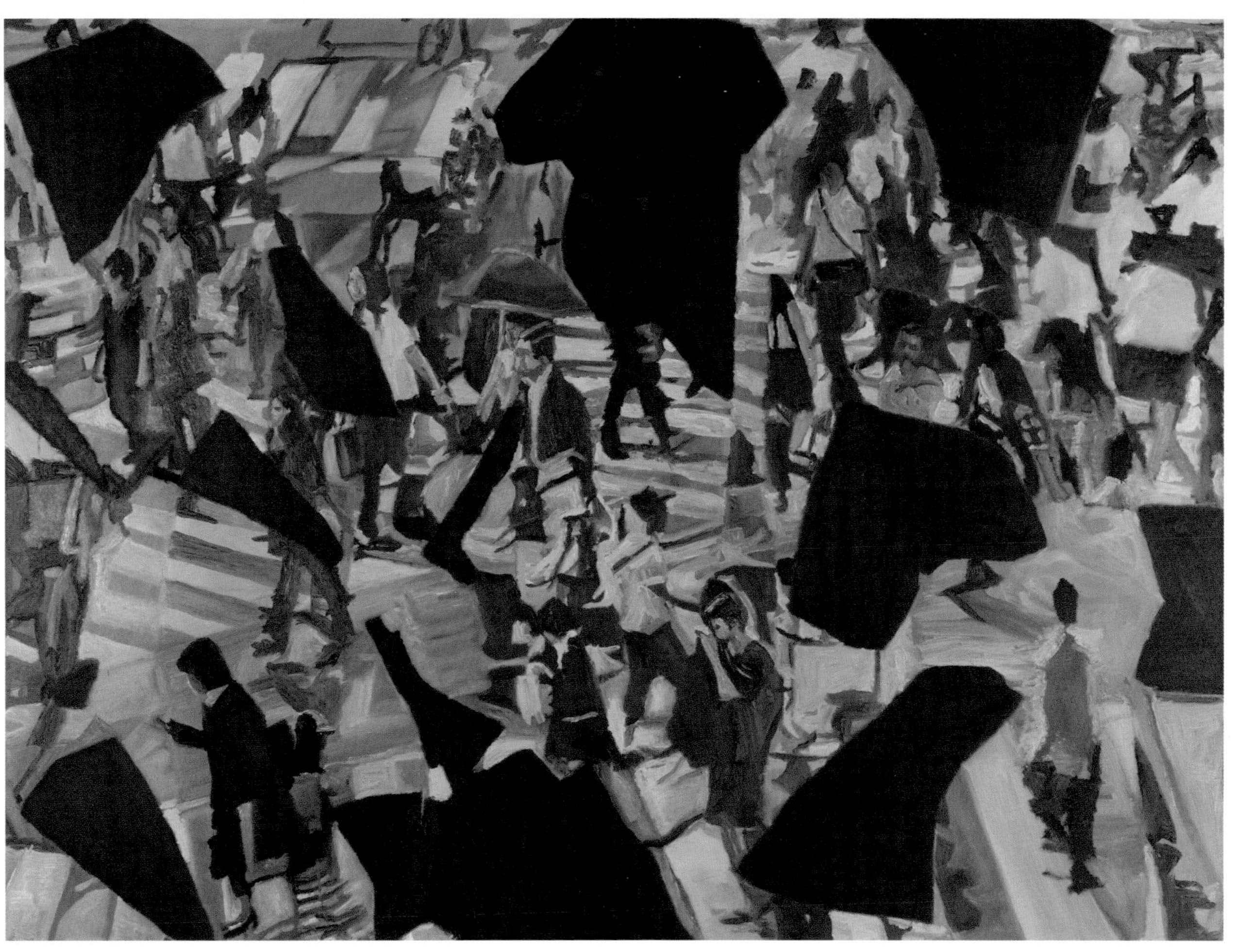

FRAGMENTATION 2017
Oil on canvas 120 x 90 cm

UNTRAMMELLED ELEMENTS: REFLECTIONS ON THE WORK OF JASMIR CREED

GRAEME GILLOCH

*"Great cities – whose incomparably sustaining and reassuring power
encloses those at work within them in an internal truce [Burgfrieden] and
lifts from them, with the view of the horizon, awareness of the ever-vigilant
elemental forces – are seen to be breached at all points by the invading
countryside. Not by the landscape, but by what is bitterest in untrammelled
nature: ploughed land, highways, night sky that the veil of vibrant redness
no longer conceals. The insecurity of even the busy areas puts the city dweller
in the opaque and truly dreadful situation in which he must assimilate,
along with isolated monstrosities from the open country, the abortions of
urban architectonics"*

(Walter Benjamin in *Selected Writings Volume 1 1913 – 1926*,
Cambridge MA: Harvard UP, 1996, p. 454). "Strength lies in
improvisation. All the decisive blows are struck left handed"
(Walter Benjamin ibid p. 447)

ARACHNE'S CITY

These two aphorisms from Walter Benjamin's famous 1926
One-Way Street [Einbahnstrasse] collection arguably capture much
of motivating source and guiding spirit of Jasmir Creed's images,
works that are principally and profoundly concerned with our
uncanny experience of the modern metropolitan environment.
The first excerpt – written, it should be noted, with a keen
sense of irony – alerts us to the interpenetration and cross-
contamination of 'first' and 'second' nature, of natural
ecosystems and human-made technosystems, to those violent
irruptions and intrusions of the one within and into the other,
and, most importantly, to their concomitant and mutual
despoliation and ruination. Moreover, it also highlights that
intense disquiet and desolation which attends those who inhabit
such blighted cityscapes and landscapes, those who must call
such *unheimlich* settings their home. The second quotation – part
of Benjamin's insistence upon the efficacy of indirection and
digress, of the unforeseen and the unintentional – is due reminder
never to underestimate the potential of the seemingly obtuse or
gauche. Not that Jasmir's images are *gauche*; far from it, it is the
Italian – not the French – that I have in mind here: these pictures
are *sinister*. They disturb us; they disquiet us; they disorient our

perceptions and destabilize our world. They are blows struck upon the tired taken-for-grantedness of mundane spaces and lives more ordinary; and they are decisive ones at that.

Vividly envisioning "the abortions of urban architectonics" and the faceless crowds who hasten past, through, across, along and within them, *Urban Forest* (The Gallery, Delta House Studios, London, January 2017) was my first encounter with Jasmir's unsettling artworks. At first, I was struck most forcefully by the sombre blue-black chiaroscuro of the large ink-on-paper pieces, with their imagining and juxtapositioning of dark, looming architectural forms and of the fine filigree of latticework *Watchers* (2016) *Flow* (2016). This is the contemporary neo-noir city as shadowscape. *Steel Webs* (2016) is exemplary and for me the stand-out piece. Here it is not so much the brute inertia of stone and concrete edifices that contrasts with the spare aerial tracery of steel and glass, but rather the human populace as a murky mass lurking, loitering below – anonymous, impersonal, funereal in attire, like a crowd that has just arrived from some nightmarish Edvard Munch painting, as if all the grotesque figures and caricatures from Ludwig Kirchner's Expressionist canvases were now newly assembled here as part of some nefarious, clandestine gathering. One can almost hear their whisperings and murmurings, the soft rhythms of their footfall, the garbled announcements relayed over some hidden tannoy system. Sound itself is as muted, as blurred as the figures. But there is nothing indistinct about the mood, the pervasive air of this ominous picture: it is pervaded by an unnamed, unspoken fear. Jasmir gives her work seemingly simple titles but these are also highly suggestive: *Steel Webs* in particular evokes one of her favourite figures, that of the spider, one of nature's most ingenious and intricate architects. The apparent fragility and delicacy of the web should not distract us from its principle purpose: it is a lethal trap for the unwary, a killing machine. And make no mistake: this is an image of menace and threat. One wonders: so where exactly is the monstrous spider that has spun these webs and are those human shadows down below its prey, or merely what is left of them, human husks, a crowd of carrion?

In imagining the labyrinthine qualities of contemporary cities, the figure of Ariadne is often invoked by cultural critics (Benjamin foremost among them): she is the cunning *flaneuse* who acts as our guide, leading us through the disorienting maze and safely out into the light. She is the personification of redemption. Jasmir draws on another, much more malign and malevolent mythological figure: not Ariadne but Arachne, the weaver, the daughter of a dyer in purple, the woman who, as punishment

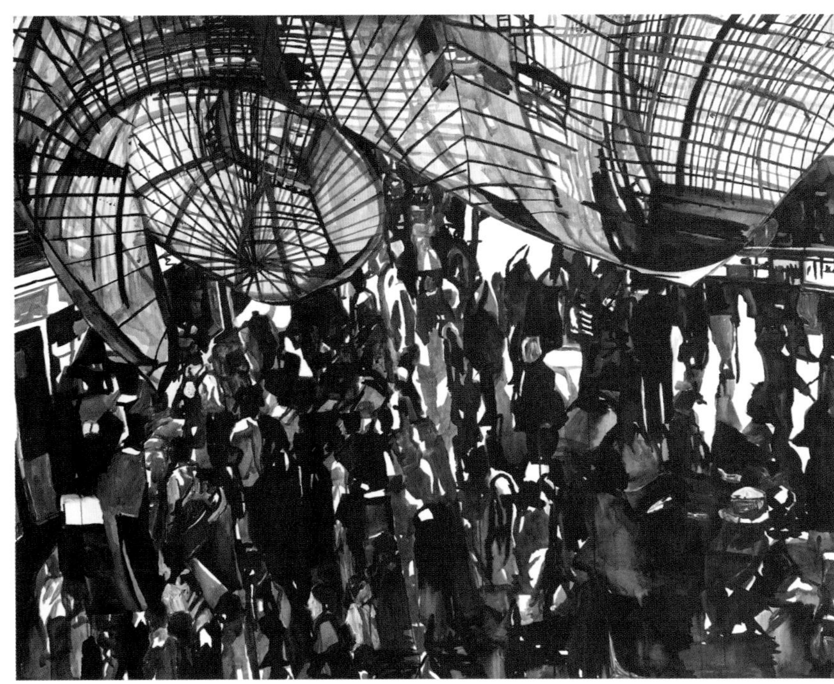

STEEL WEBS 2016
Ink on paper 150 x 120 cm

for her hubris, is transformed into a spider by Athena, goddess
of wisdom. It is Arachne who patiently awaits us in this urban
forest; or perhaps we sit with her, we *become* her even, high
up in her metallic mesh with eyes trained upon those beneath,
watching and waiting, biding the time. Arachne is a figure of
patient predation.

Urban Forest: the very title presents us with the implosion
of the natural world and the built environment. And they are home
not only to our primal arachnid fears, but to the hypermodern
metropolitan malaise of alienation, anonymity, dislocation,
de-personalization, isolation, paranoia and acrophobia. *The Fall*
(2015) appears to depict a whirling figure who has simply had
enough and now tumbles headlong down into the vanishing
point of the picture between two twisting skyscrapers. This is
part of another monochromatic series of pen and charcoal on
paper images which simultaneously resemble aerial views of
some sprawling, fractured city spread out below *Interweave* (2015)
and provoke a dizzying sense of the vertiginous. Circular patterns
and spiralling, swirling forms seem to produce a vortex at the
centre of these pictures towards which one is irresistibly drawn
by centripetal forces, into which one disappears without trace
Funnelscape (2015), *Mirage* (2015).

Working from cut-outs and photomontage compositions, Jasmir's paintings also envision the sinister cityscape by means of broken planes and panels, jagged and irregular, with polymorphous forms inserted, intruded, abutted, conjoined, imploded into and within them. Part monochromatic, part a pale wash (sometimes acrylic, sometimes oils) of washed-out colour (oranges, reds, blues), these are not so much shards or fragments – such terms suggest something fragile like the tesserae of a mosaic or sharp like glass splinters – as crude chunks, lumps, blocks or boulders of buildings, masonry, railway tracks, roadways, steps, pavements, root systems, walk-ways, all peopled by yet more faceless pedestrians crossing back and forth *Flood* (2016), *Swarm* (2016), *Dystoban* (2016), *Structures and Maps* (2015), *Entrancement* (2016). It is as if the entire city has been blasted apart and these are the left-overs, the remnants and the rubble, now compacted together into rough and incongruous composites, sites of dereliction and decay inhabited by sleepwalkers. For Jasmir, the task of the artist is to rework the waste and waste-lands of the city, to recognise and reconfigure the ruinscape, and to represent the lost souls who roam it. We are forlorn, forgotten and forgetful forest dwellers.

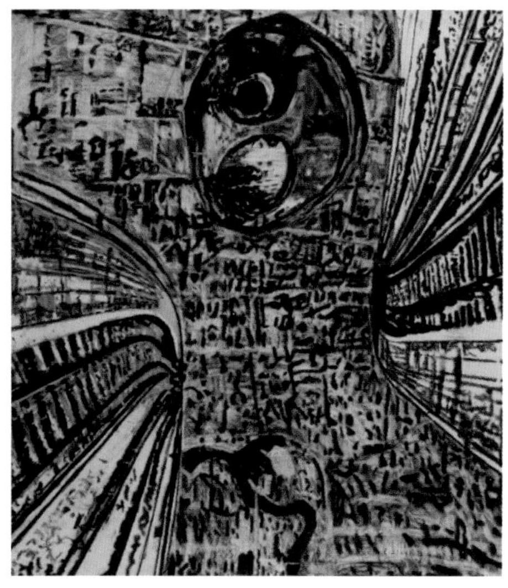

THE FALL 2015
Charcoal on paper 215 x 150 cm

Jasmir's new show *Dystopolis* rekindles her preoccupation with the urban uncanny through reiterating and rejigging earlier motifs, adding new and original elements to her visual vocabulary, injecting fresh colours and tones, broadening the scope and scale of paper and canvas. In so doing, she moves back and forth between the apparently generic cityscape imagined in *Urban Forest* (essentially a composite of Manchester and London) and a particular and identifiable one – indeed, the one that is hosting her exhibition: Liverpool.

Sometimes Lost (2018), for example, presents us once again with Jasmir's favourite theme – the metropolitan crowd – but with a Liverpudlian inflection. Here they walk towards and away from the viewer, into and out of the canvas, while above them soars not the spidery creations of *Steel Webs* but rather a curious central metallic column, ice-blue and silver grey, which splays out into what could be supporting arches and vaults of some colossal edifice or even, more prosaically, some kind of watertower.

This painting is a *trompe d'oeil*. Turned upside down, the architectural centrepiece is immediately revealed and recognised as an image of Liverpool's famous Metropolitan Cathedral, the affectionately termed 'wigwam'. Set against a fiery yellow-orange background and framed by the black silhouettes of industrial towers and oil burners, the outline of this iconic building is also evident in the grey-white central panel of *Vessel* (2018). Pedestrians here seem to be ascending the Cathedral's central tower, the gridwork of paving stones suggesting both steps to be climbed and an exterior of manifold glass panes.

Altar Island (2018) takes us down to the city's waterfront and presents us with a playful double spatial reversal. On the far side of the Albert Dock, the architecture of the city is turned upside down as it is reflected a pale yellowy orange in the murky Merseyside waters. The characteristically monochromatic panel comprising the foreground features a few faceless figures to the left apparently attending to various stone features occupying the centre and right of the canvas: an altar of some kind, some broken statuary, a piece of masonry. In a second inversion, Jasmir has taken these elements from within the Metropolitan Cathedral and strewn them on the dockside, turning the building inside out so to speak. It is not just 'some times' that are 'lost' in these works, but some spaces too – spaces out of place, displaced, loci gone walkabout, somewhere now elsewhere.

True, Jasmir's new works stay loyal to her tried and tested montage technique such that the canvas appears transformed into a broken windowpane. Moreover, the anonymous, agitated urban crowd drained of colour remains her *leitmotif*. These pedestrians appear either as a smeary blur of soft grey tones as if seen through fine, misty drizzle *Fragmentation*, (2017) or, occasionally, as black-clad figures scurrying hither and thither *Urban Flux*, (2017). But something decisive has changed: her passers-by now appear as if surrounded, encircled, besieged by something truly monstrous, overwhelming, unstoppable, irresistible, remorseless, unfathomable: by untrammelled Nature. We are no longer lost in some vast 'urban forest' but rather losing ground to the encroachments of another, more forceful and formidable flora altogether: giant stems, leaves, blooms, lily pads and root systems which Baudelaire most assuredly did not have in mind when he named his cycle of poems *Les fleurs du mal* but for which the designation 'the flowers of evil' seems most apt. In a series of works from 2017, among them *Through the Foliage*, *Fauna Mist*, *Pastoralax*, *Naturban*, *Dystopiature*, *City Pads*, Jasmir presents us with the collision of two highly invasive species, a violent coming together captured in the linguistic play and neologisms of the titles themselves. And in this clash of worlds, the humans are not faring well. By nesting the fragments of the cityscape within these blooming, twisting, writhing, proliferating vegetal masses, Jasmir ensures a two-fold effect: on the one hand, it creates the sense of the city being swallowed up, or suffocated, or swamped by some superabundant plant-life; on the other, it positions the viewer of the image in amongst the foliage itself. We are peering through the gargantuan leaves, peeking between the behemothic blooms. We are witnesses to the revenge of Nature, to the coming of the triffids, from *their* vantage point. The observer of these scenes is no longer an arachnid ensconced high up in the canopy but hidden down amongst the undergrowth turned overgrowth, a praying mantis, stealthy, silent. We are closing in upon the humans. They are the ones who exist now only as 'isolated monstrosities'. And we spy on them no longer through a cracked window, but through the fractures in the concrete wrought by the mute but inexorable power of relentless root systems. What is perhaps most striking about these recent works is Jasmir's unexpected use of colour: the monochromism of the urban fragments is now intensified by the bright hues of the vegetation which now engulf them: sunset reds and oranges, shades of crimson and violet, all manner of vegetal greens and yellows. For, rest assured, in experimenting with a new palette for these images, she has not abandoned her fundamental preternatural tone and mood. Far from it: the vivid colours on show here serve to compound rather than diminish the sinister qualities of the flora. The spider may be the stuff of our nightmares, but how much more unnerving this bizarre profusion and confusion of the seemingly innocent. These flowers are a bouquet presented left handed. That is how Nature strikes its blows.

The garish garlands serve to emphasise the sense of enclosure and entrapment of the central figure. This in turn replays and gives fresh inflection to another of Jasmir's earlier motifs: the vortex. And here one comes upon two works which seem to suggest a fresh point of departure for her work – a 'new sensibility' would be an exaggeration; let us call it, a more playful, more optimistic inflection. In *Whirlpool* (2018) a spiral staircase or stairwell leads down into a fragment of a swimming pool filled with swimmers and bathers suitably attired in bright summer hues. Yes, there is the vertiginous and the acrophobic, but the fall here is not into nothingness and the void but rather a dive into water. A curious image, but a softer landing. And then there is *Pool of Life* (2018), a painting inspired by a dream recounted by the Swiss analytical psychologist Carl Jung. Here there is another aquatic central panel but this time it resembles not so much a populated lido as a humble puddle in a city street, the lingering remainder and reminder of the rains which fall torrentially upon the crowds depicted to the right. It is a simple thing to be sure, but its glassy waters reflect the now cloudless blue sky above. It is as if a piece of the heavens had fallen to earth. A puddle, a pool of life, a living pool; Liverpool, Liverpudlian. Perhaps this city has brought a fleeting fragment of the celestial to brighten Jasmir's sinister cities. Perhaps, as the water-diviner of dystopolis, she has found us a wishing well.

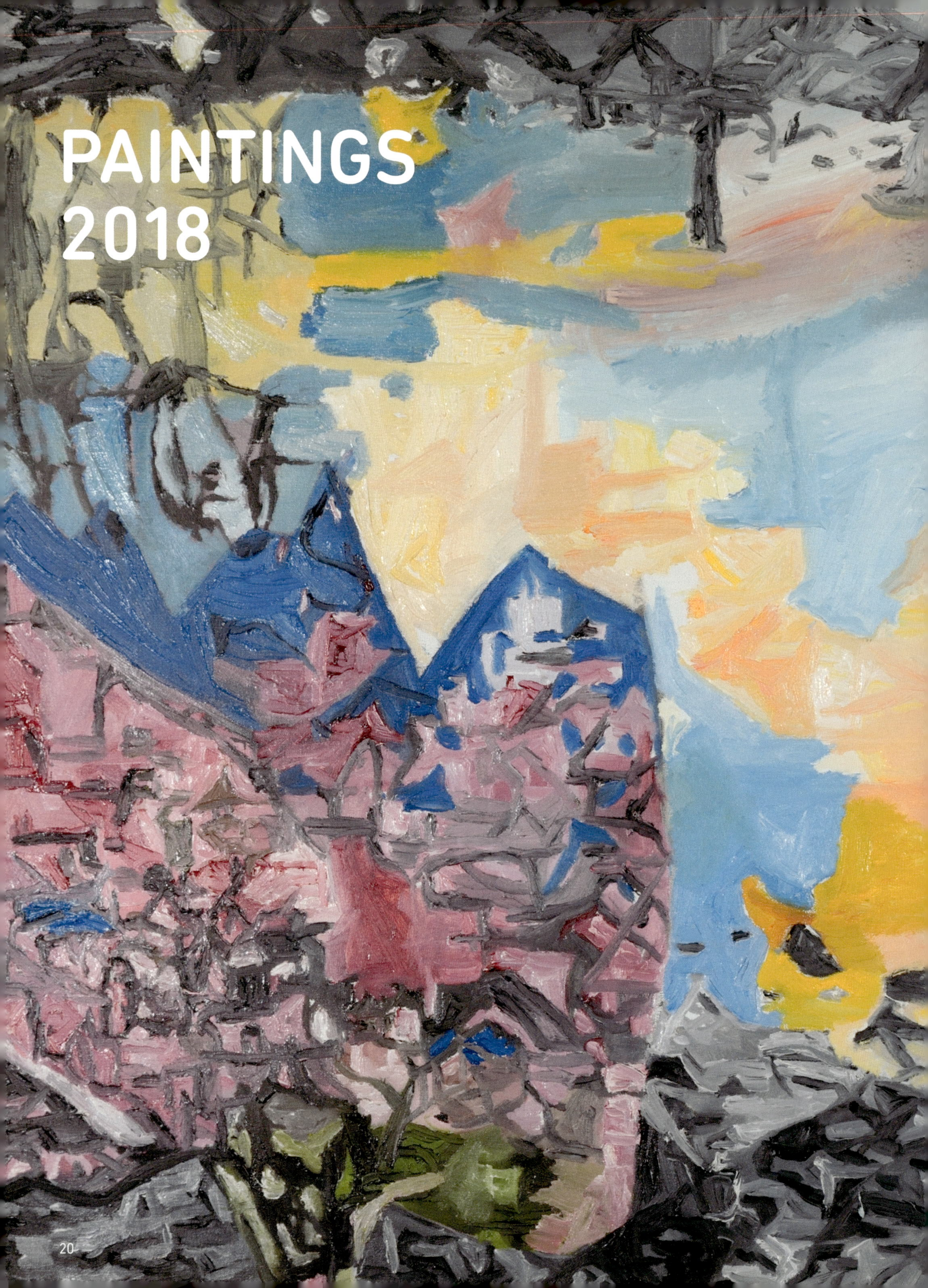
PAINTINGS
2018

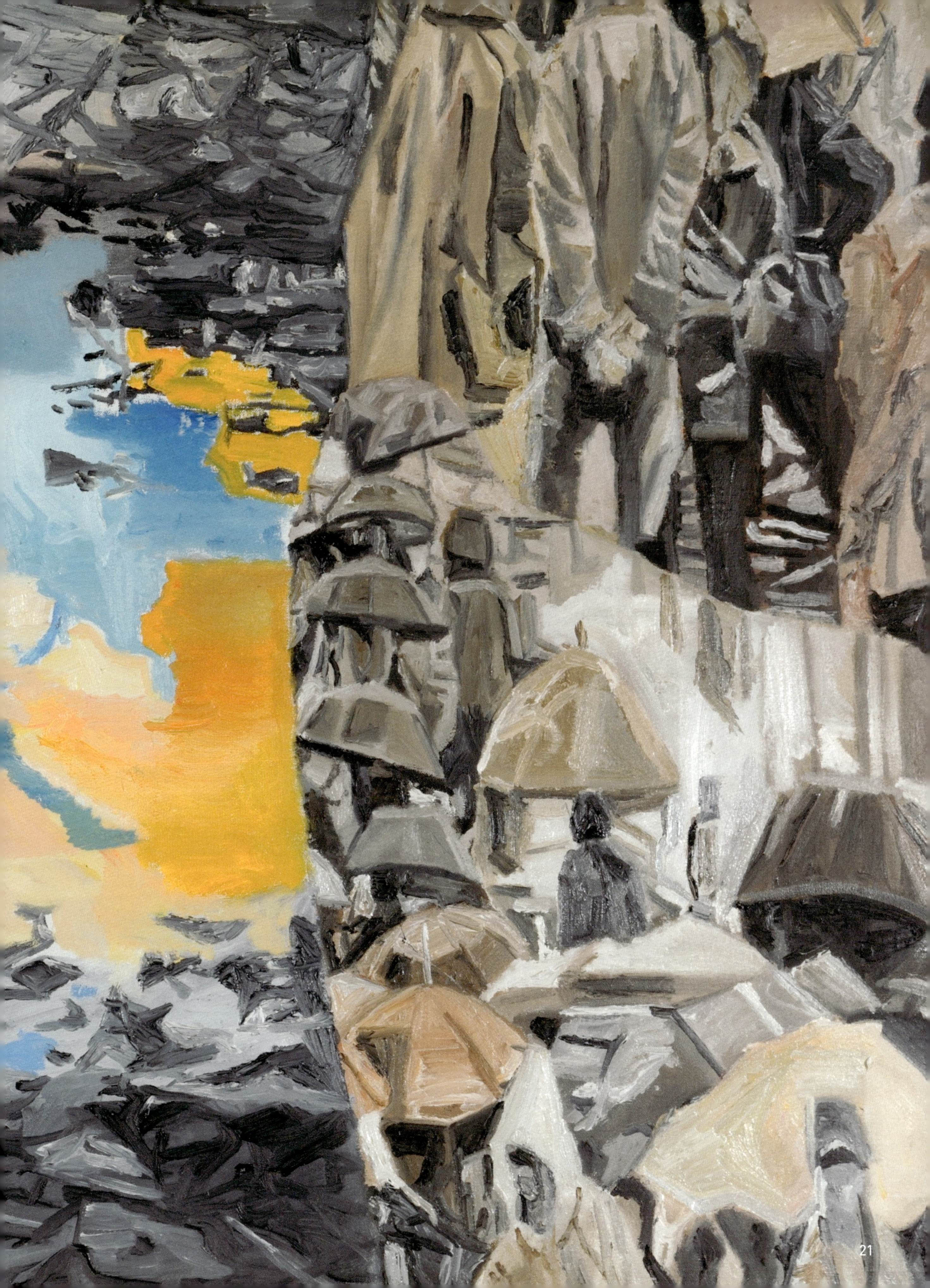

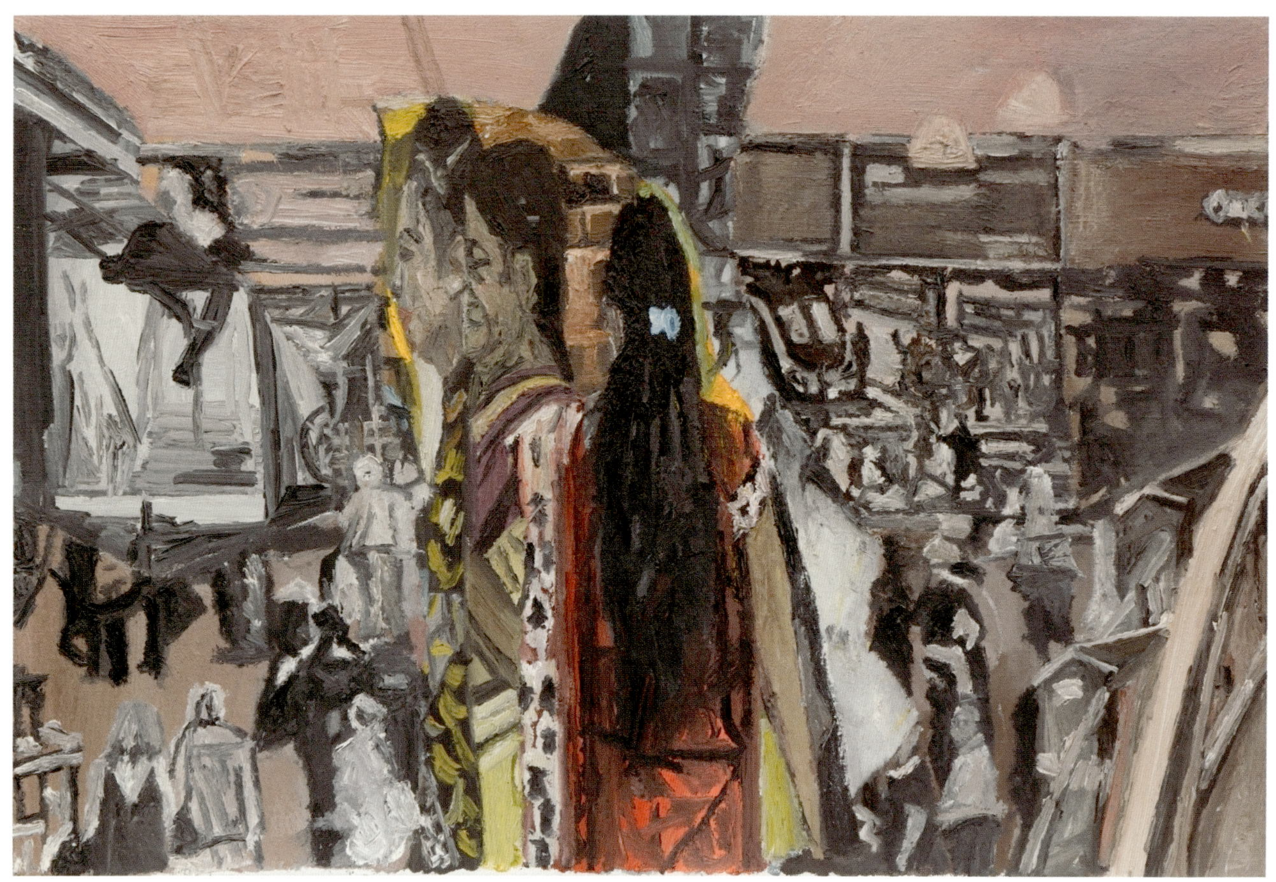

THREE 2018
Oil on canvas 60 x 40 cm

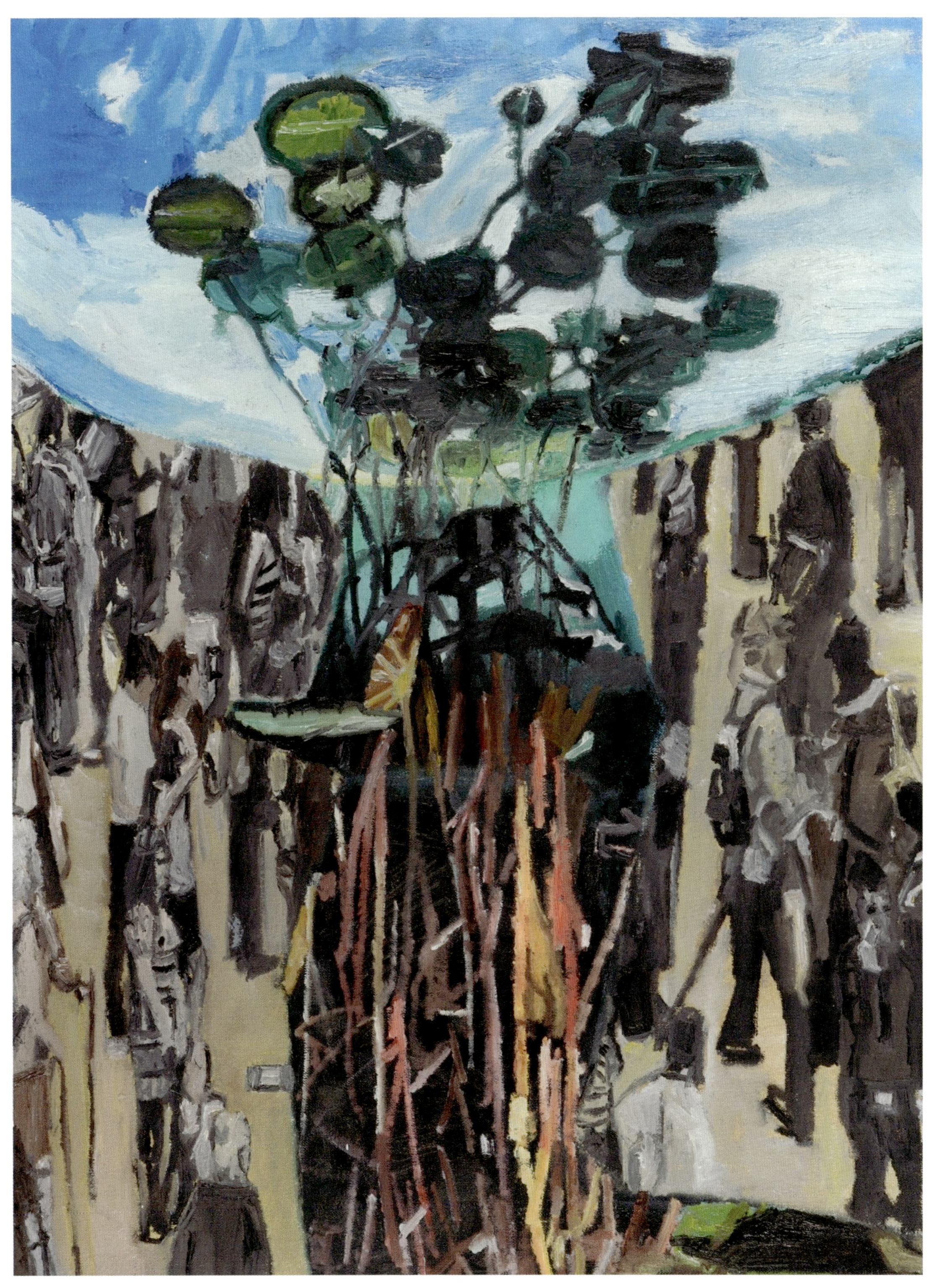

CITY PADS 2017
Oil on canvas 60 x 40 cm

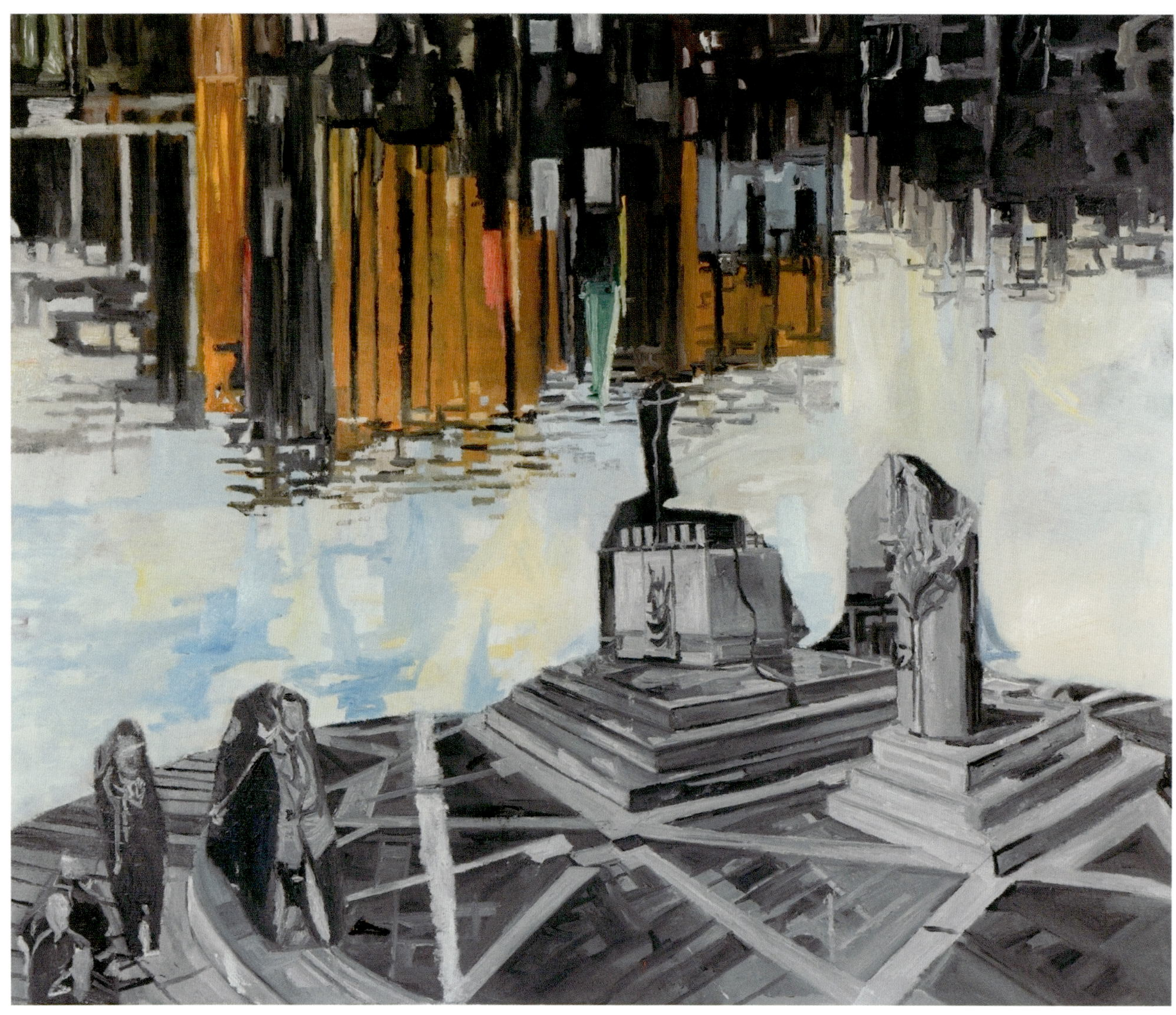

ALTAR ISLAND 2018
Oil on canvas 120 x 90 cm

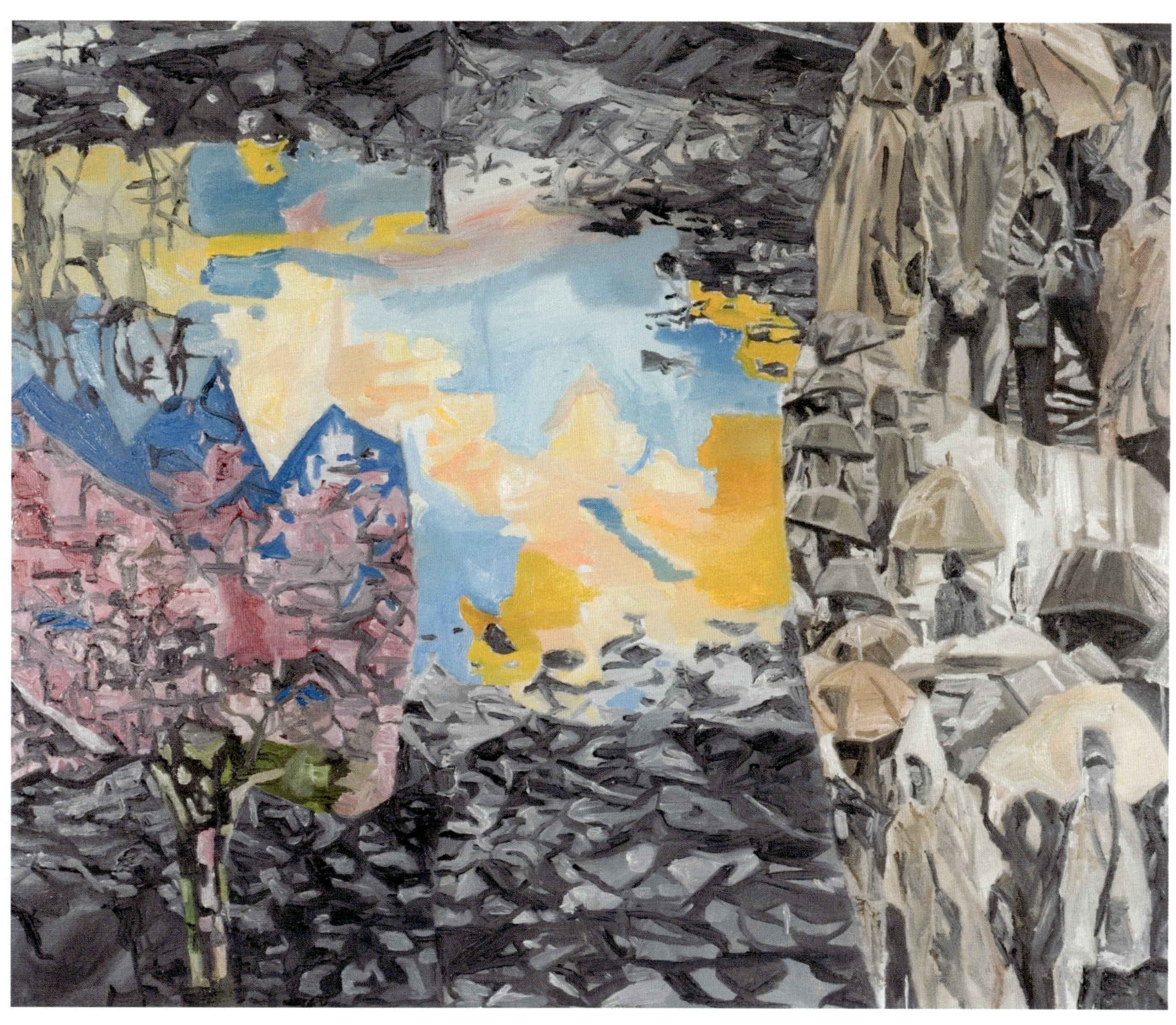

POOL OF LIFE 2018
Oil on canvas 120 x 90 cm

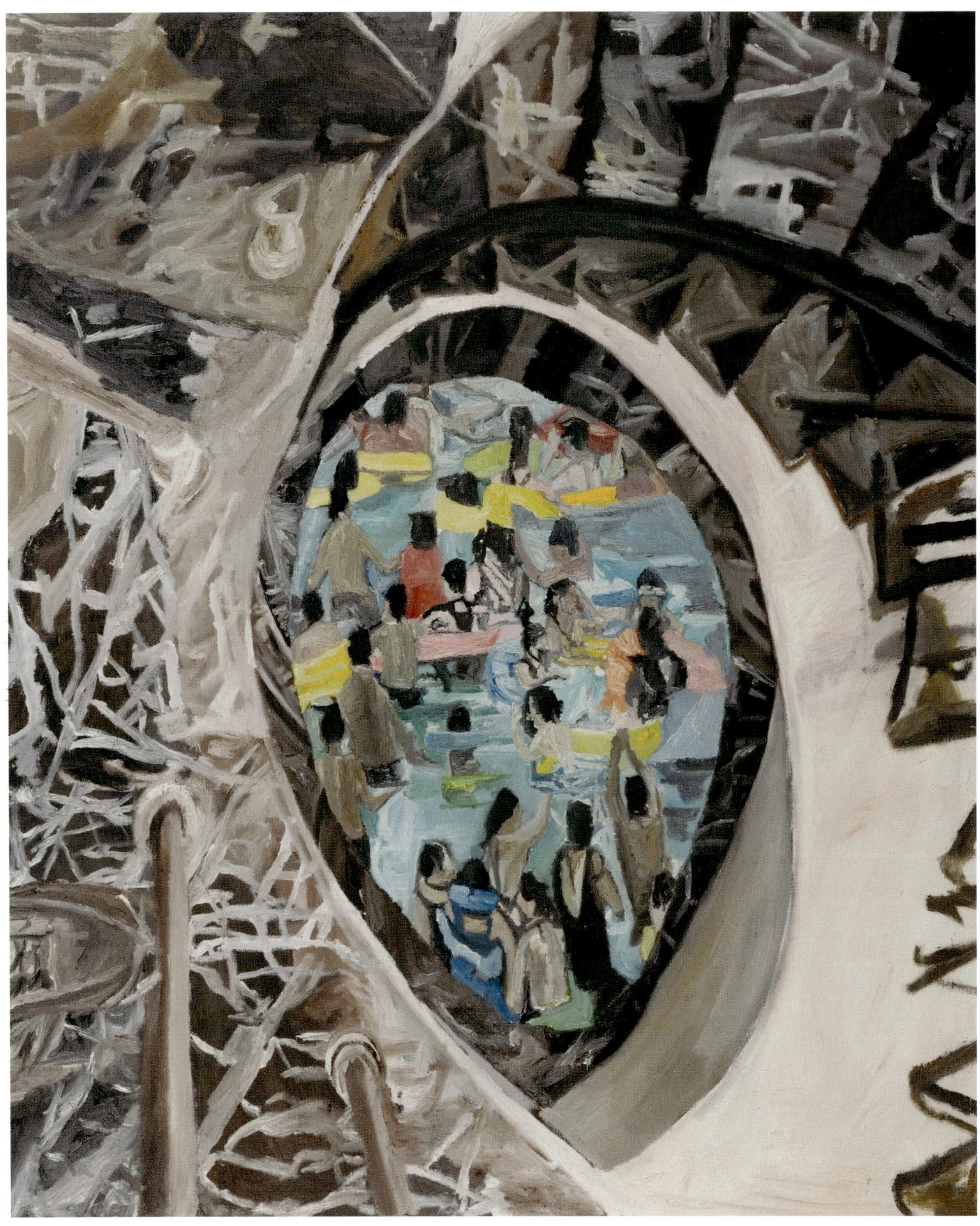

WHIRLPOOL 2018
Oil on canvas 120 x 90 cm

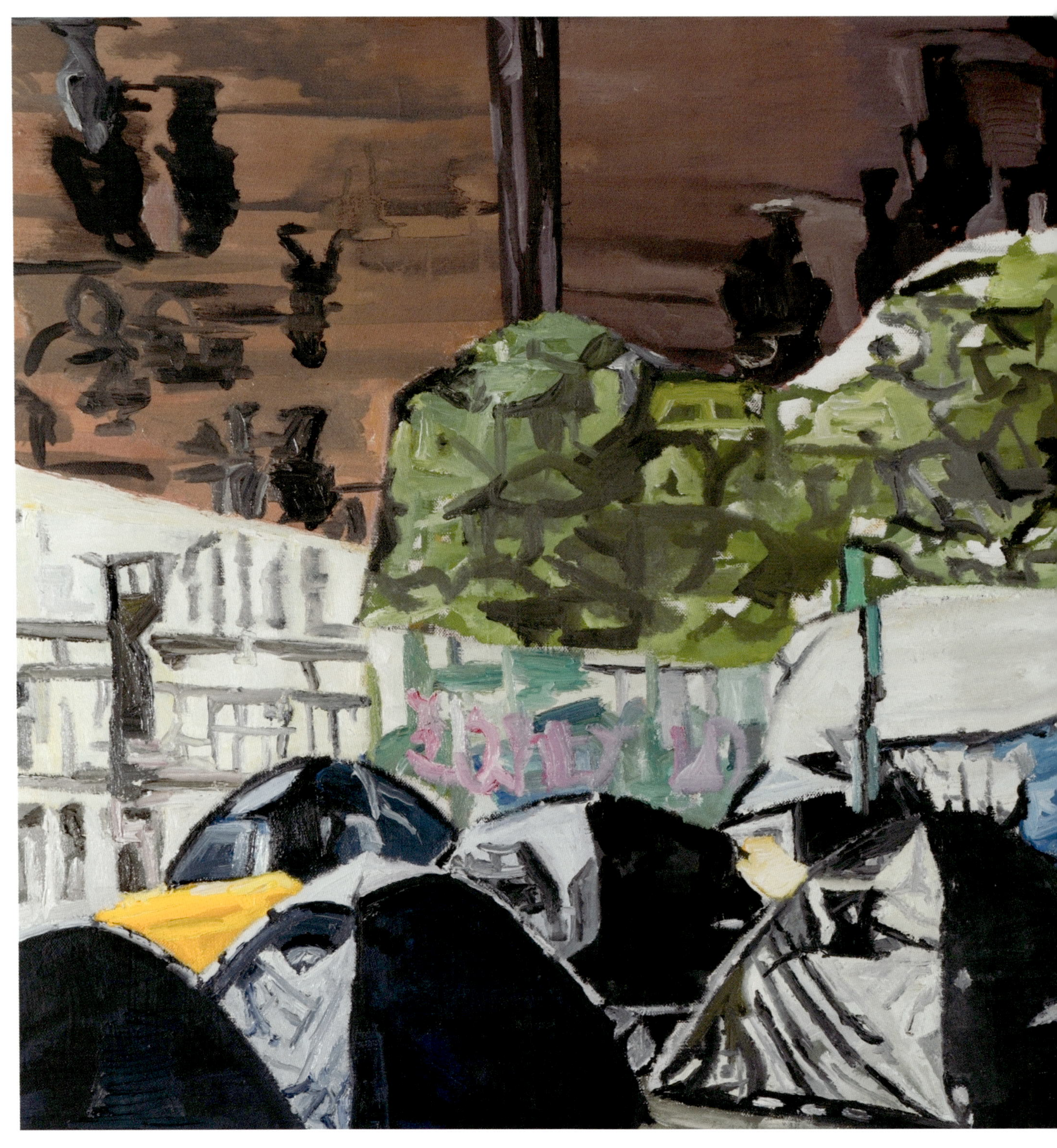

UNDERCAMP 2018
Oil on canvas 100 x 65 cm

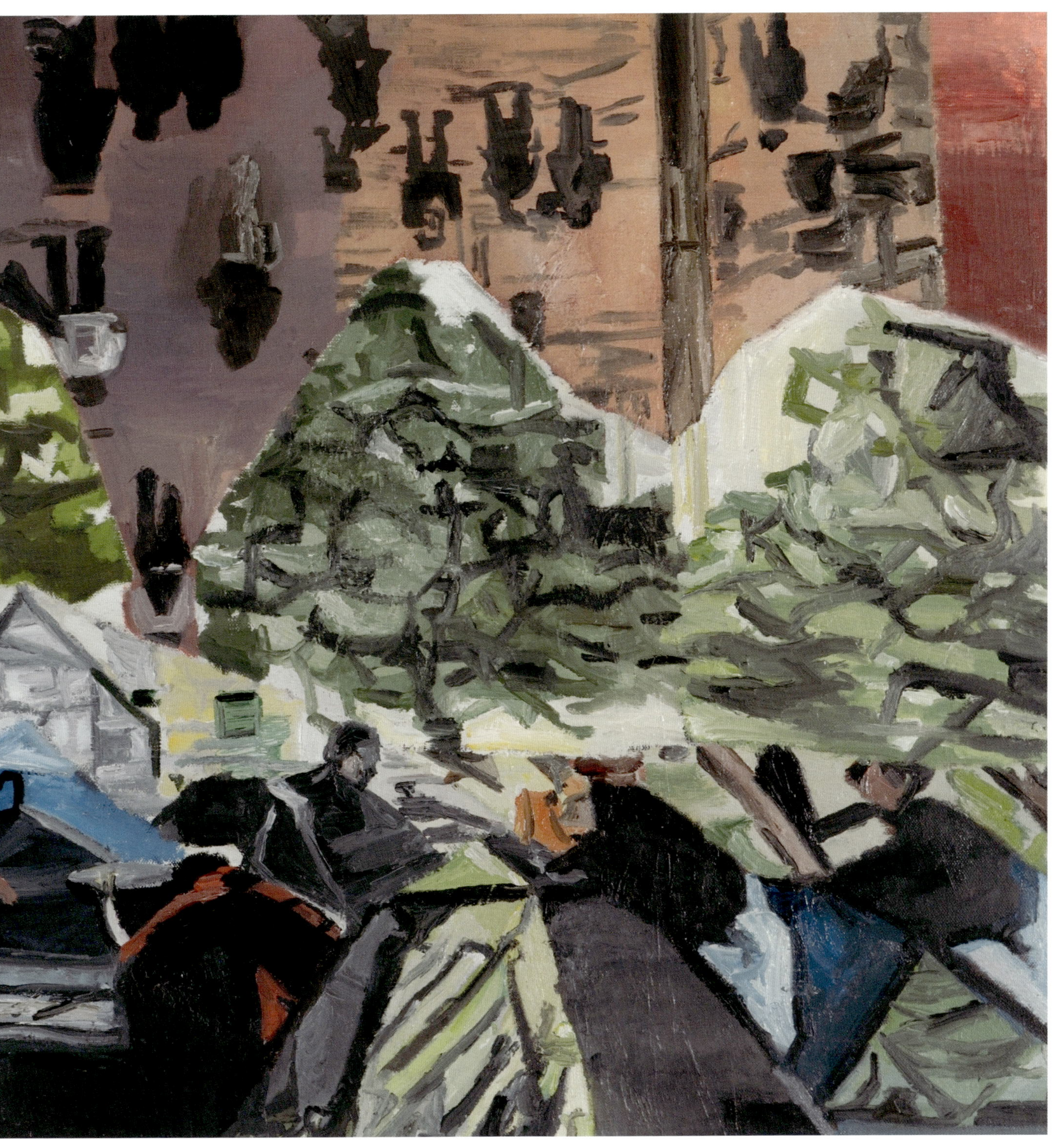

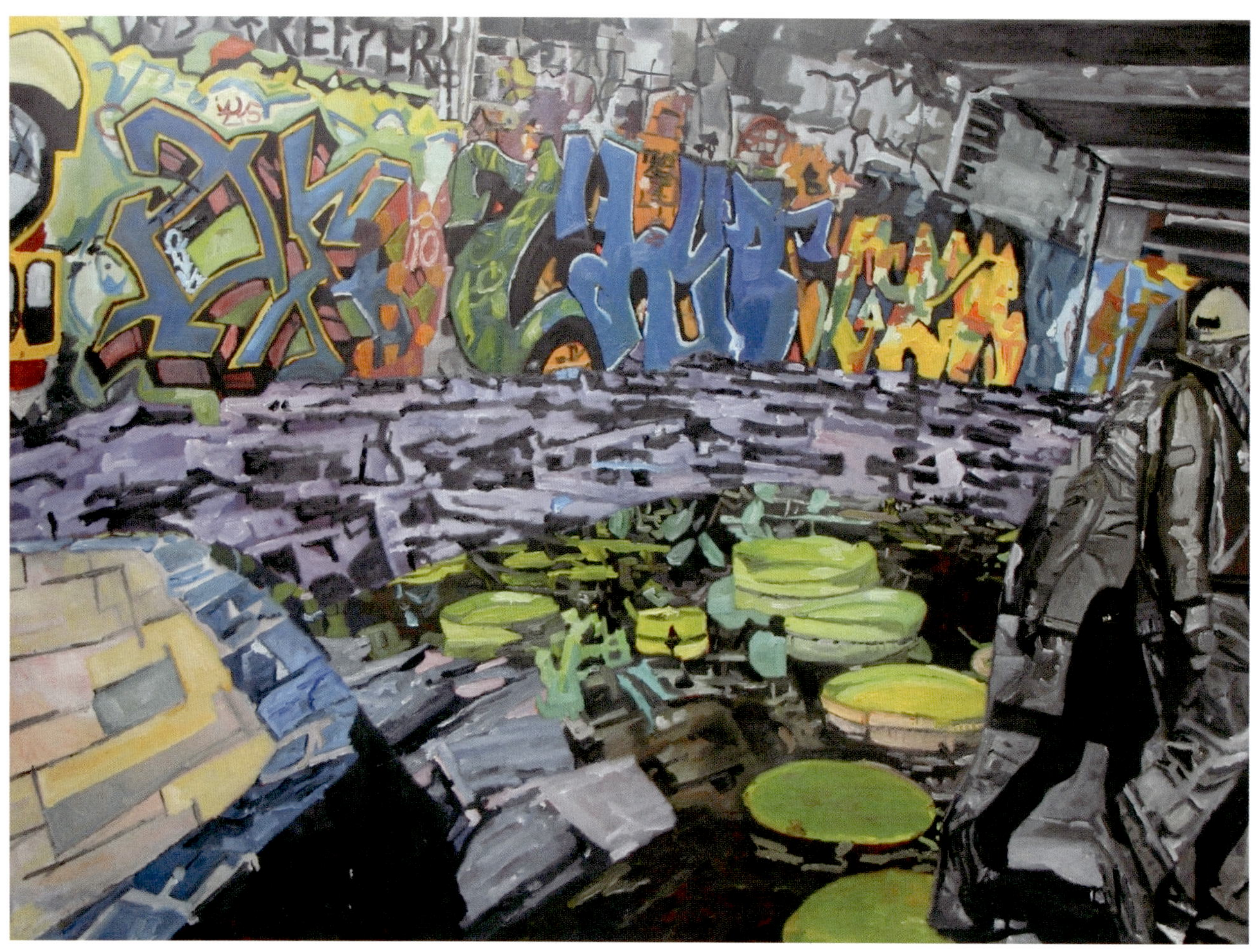

UNDERPASS 2018
Oil on canvas 213 x 152 cm

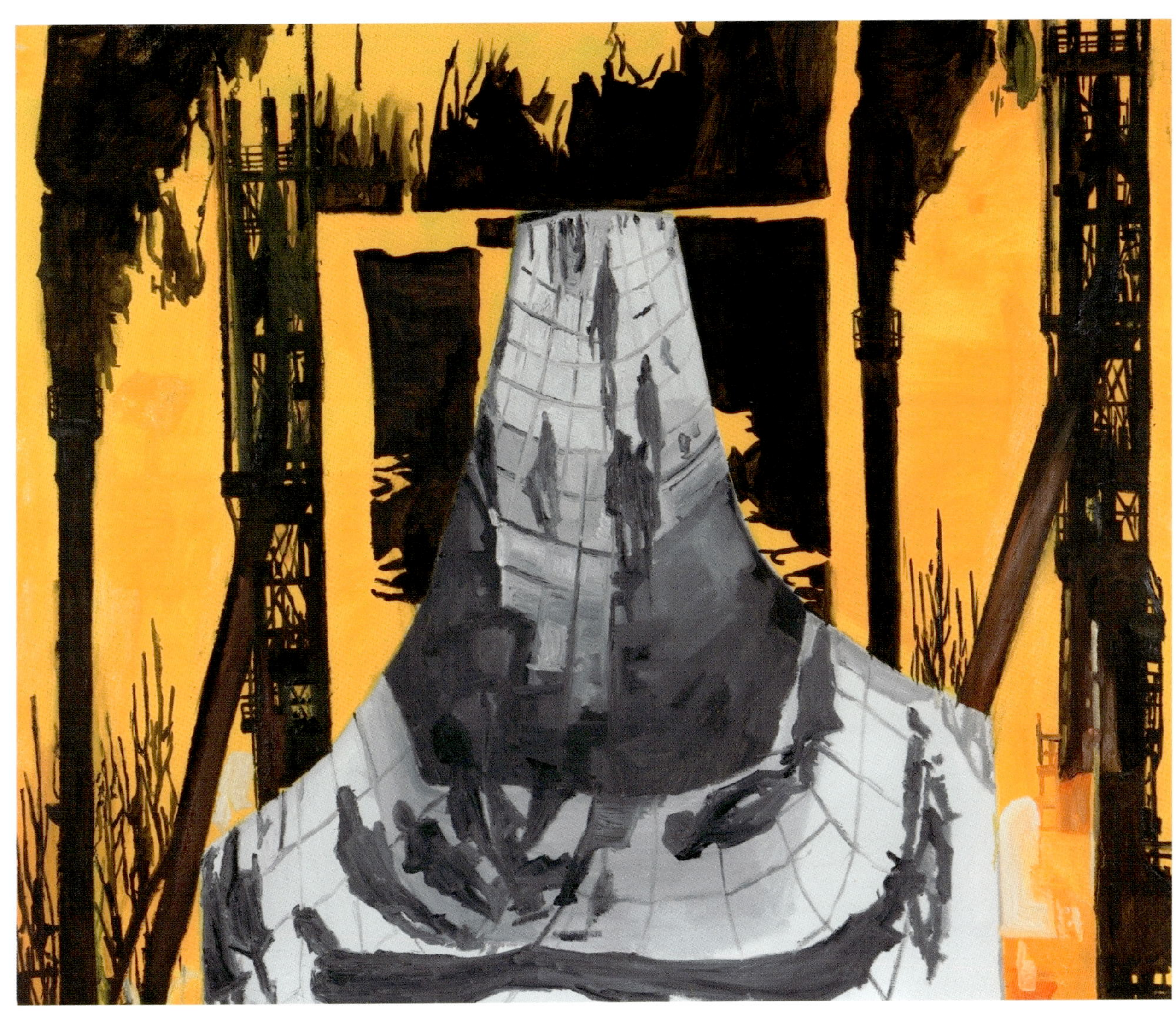

VESSEL 2018
Oil on canvas 120 x 90 cm

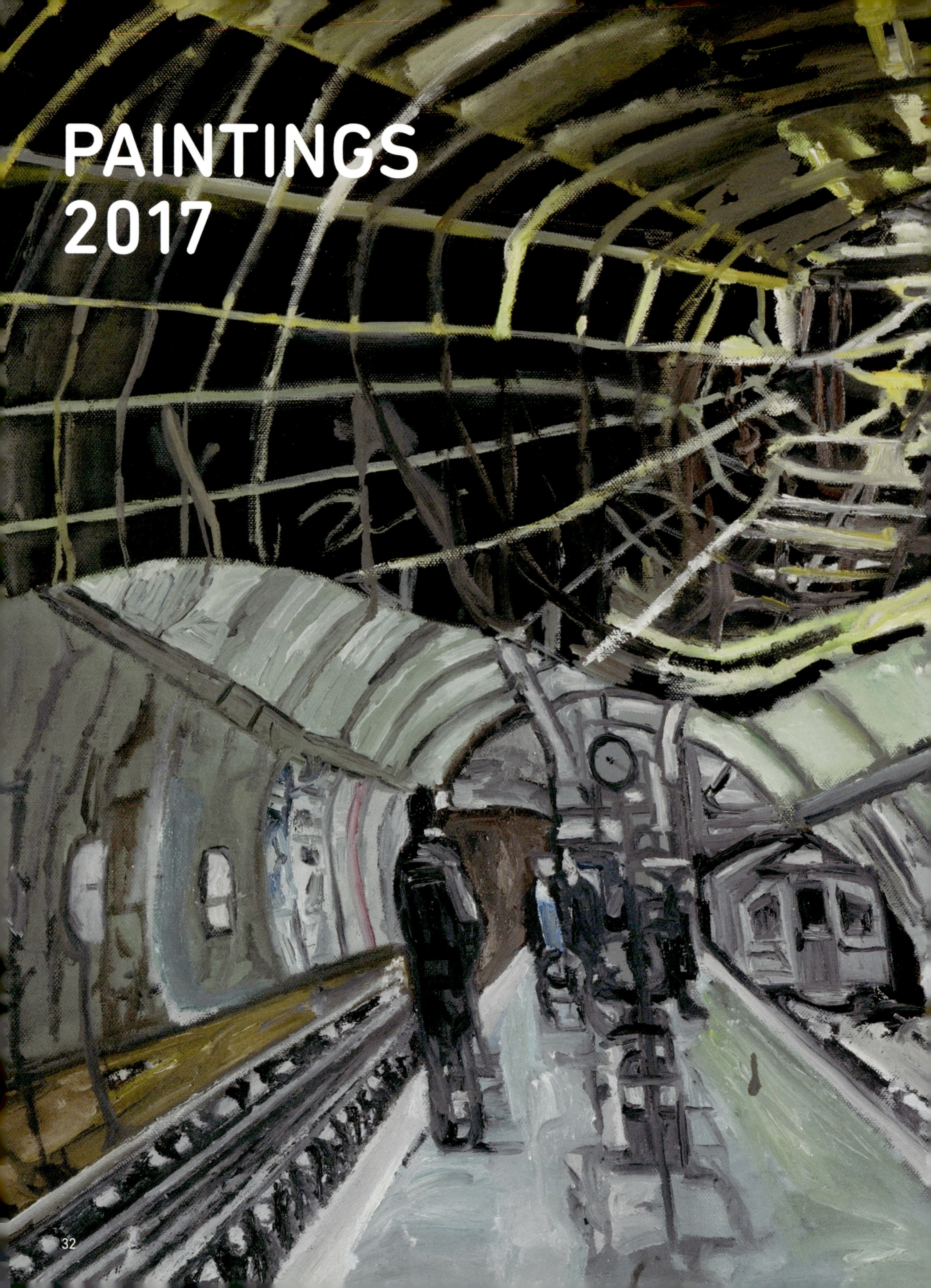
PAINTINGS
2017

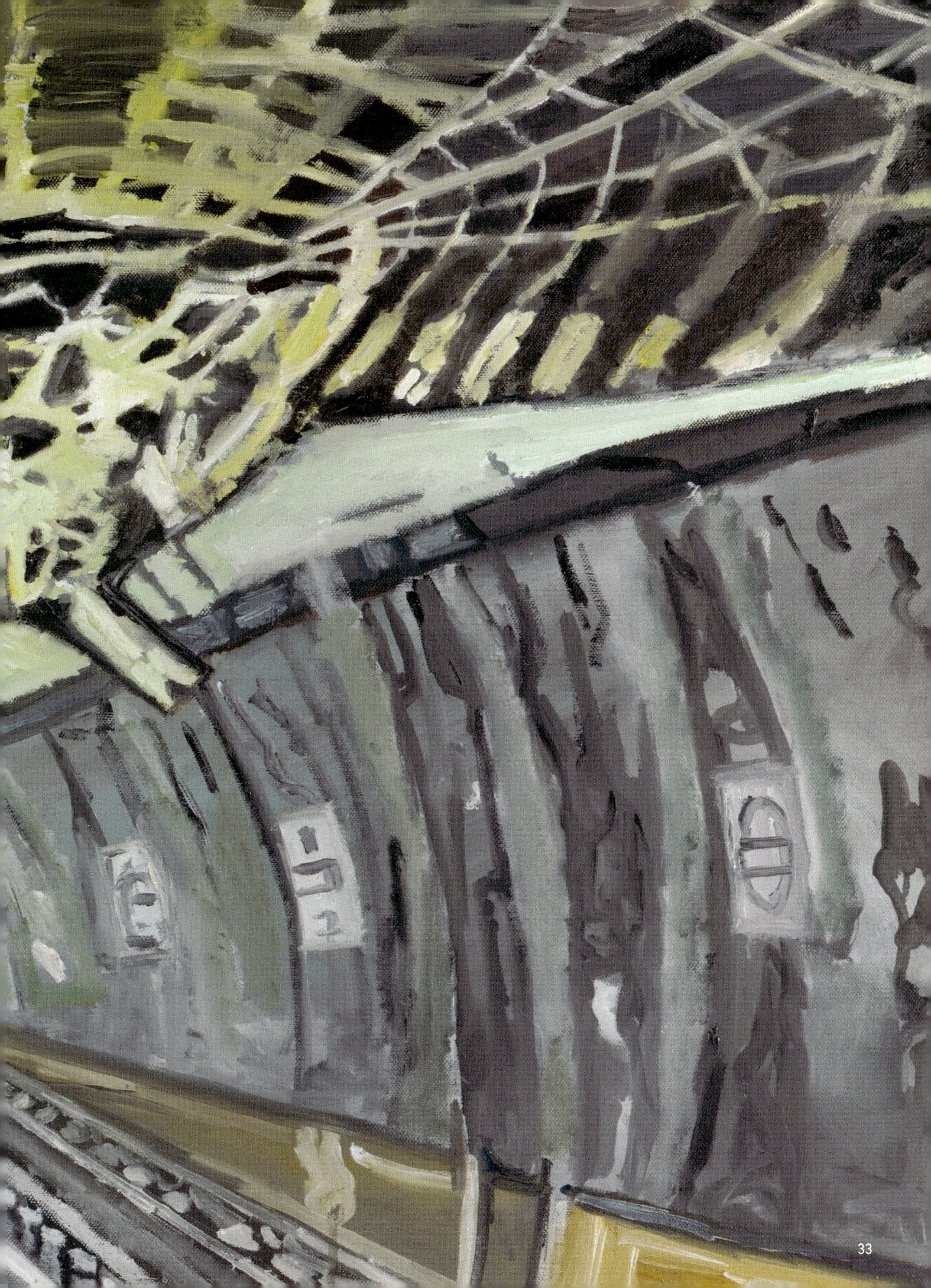

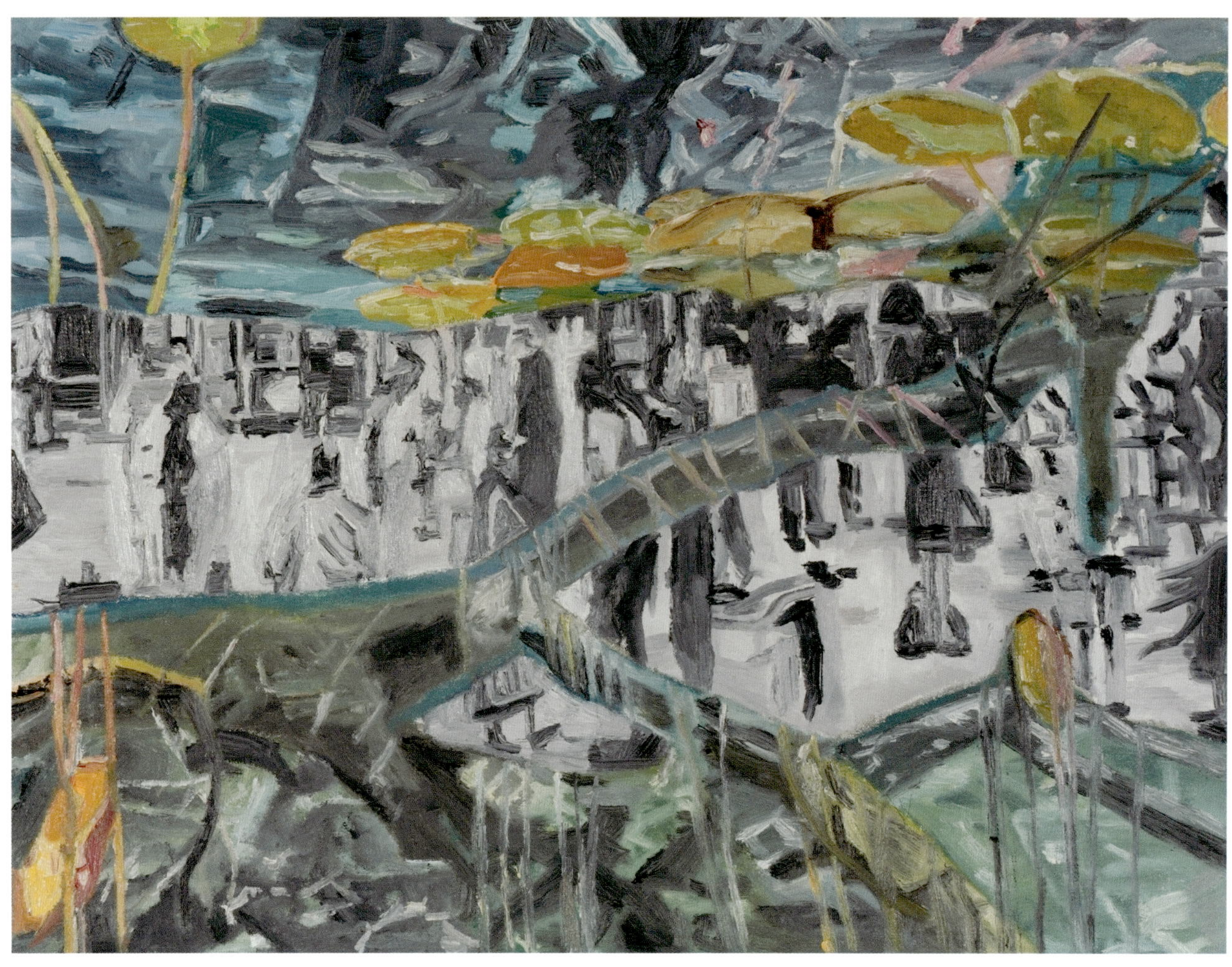

AQUATANK 2017
Oil on canvas 60 x 40 cm

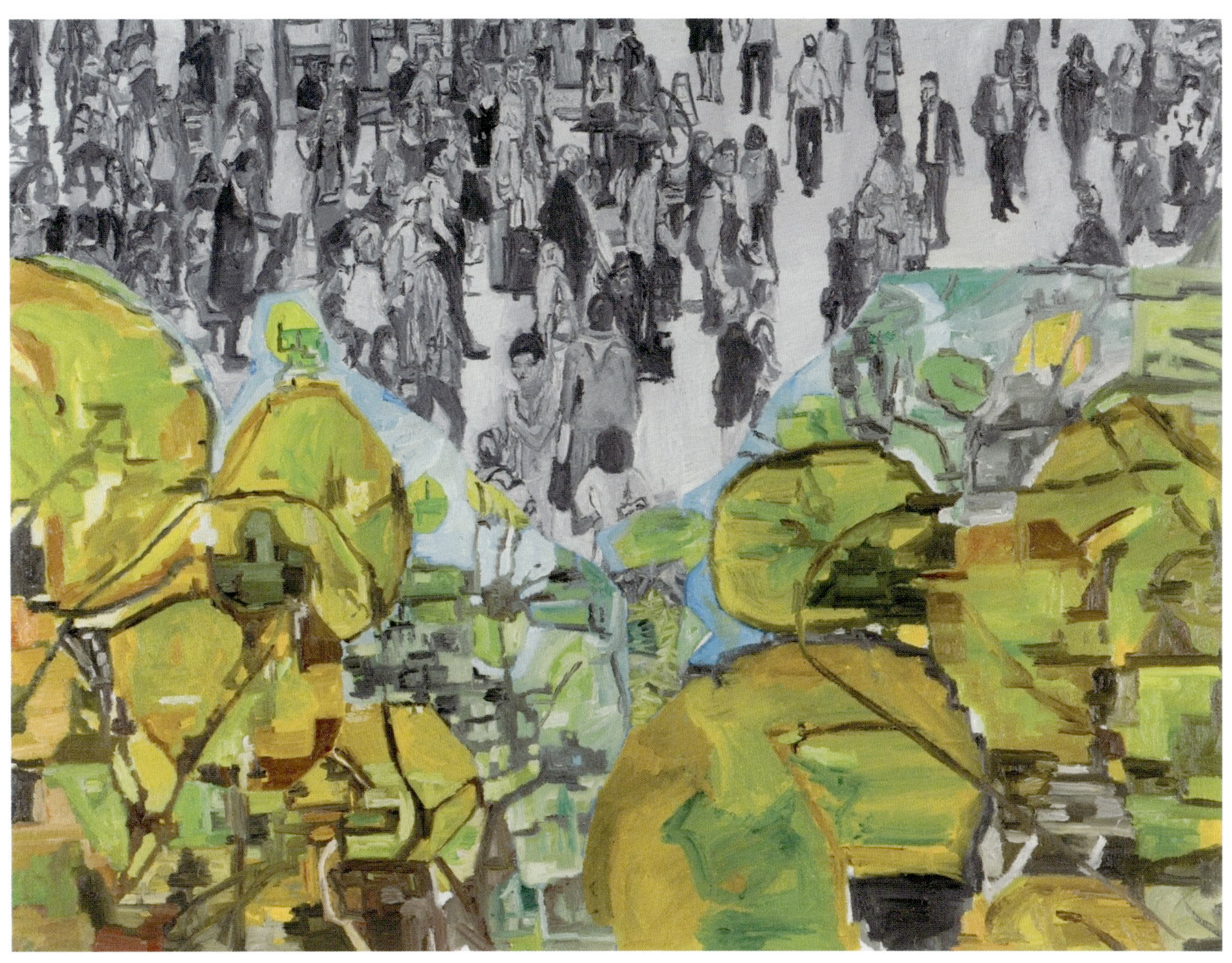

PASTORALUX 2017
Oil on canvas 120 x 90 cm

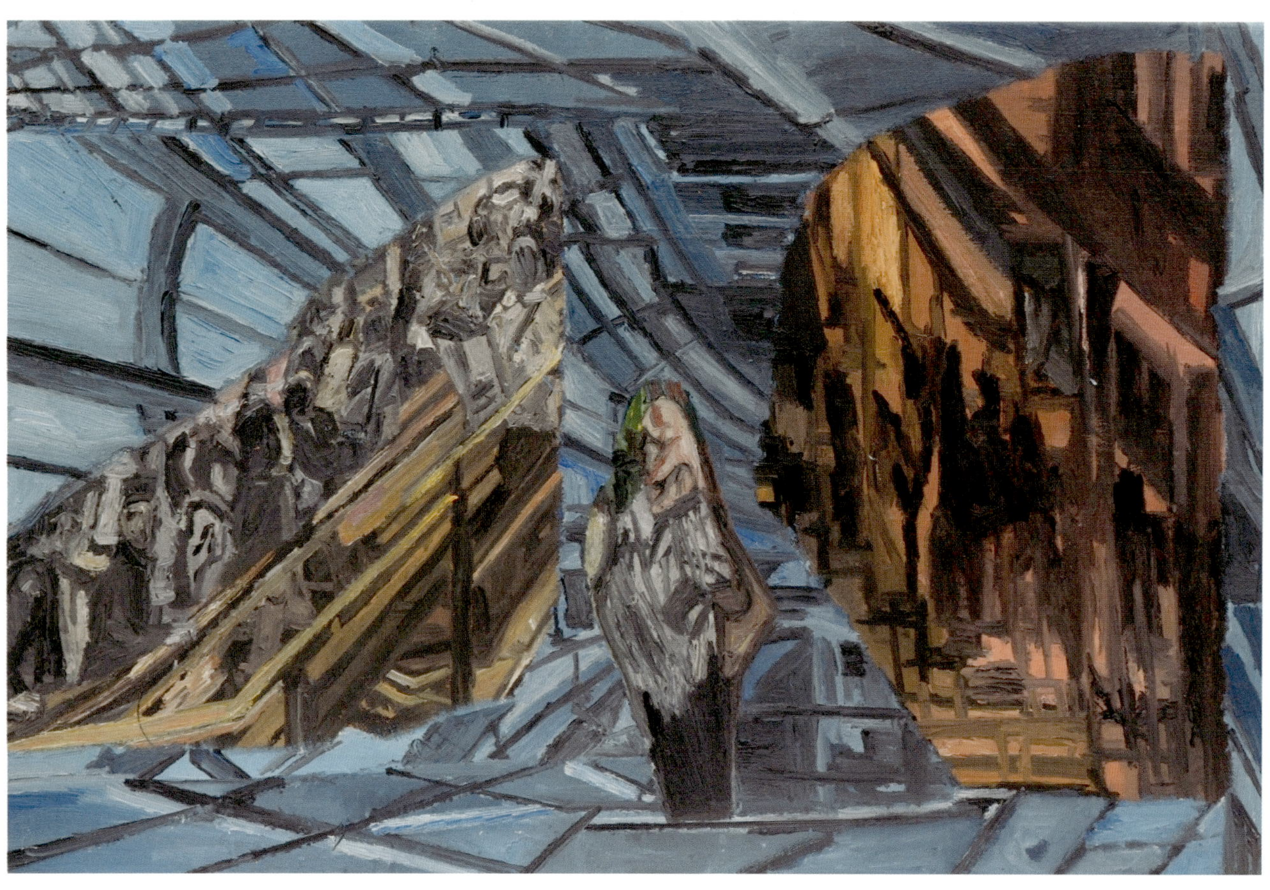

WAITING AT THE STATION 2017
Oil on canvas 60 x 40 cm

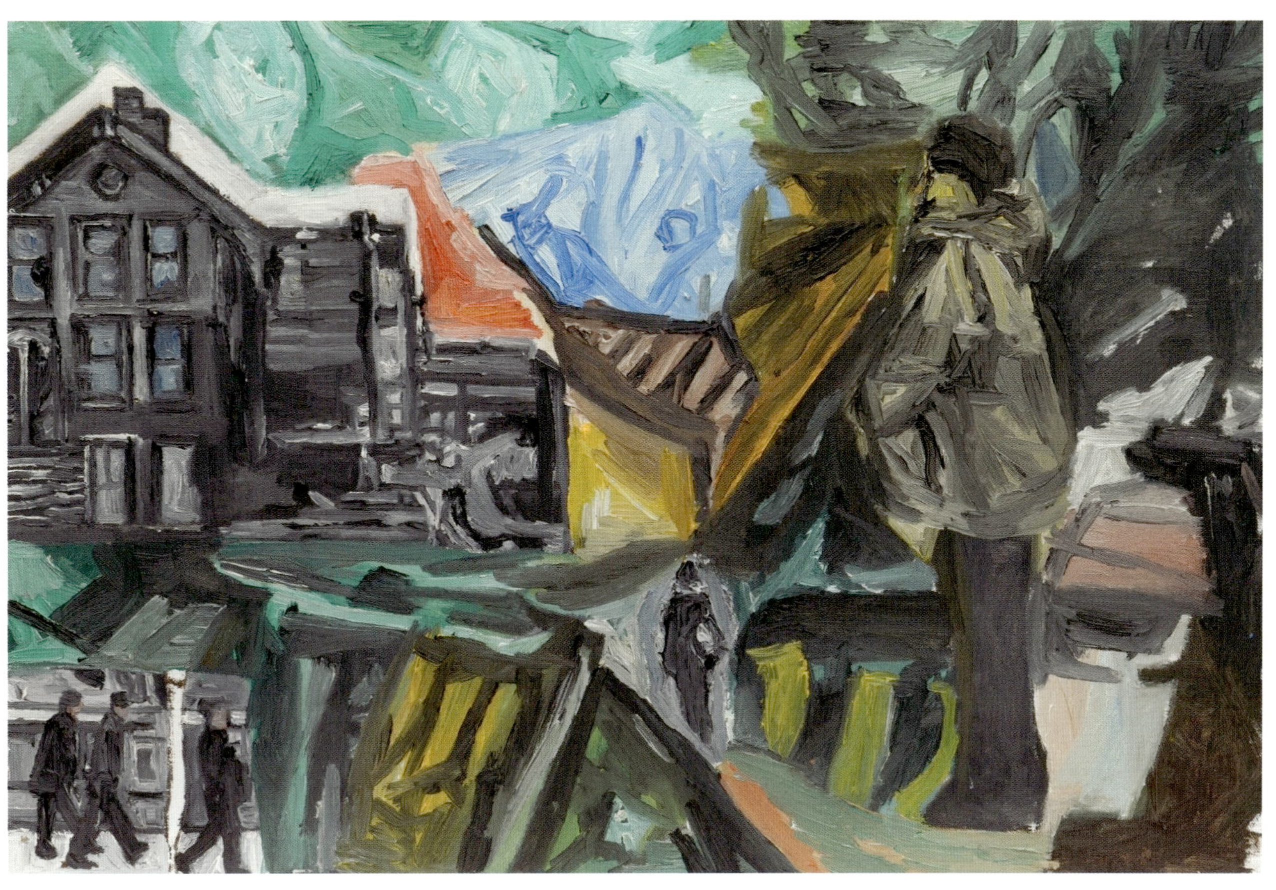

SKETCH 2017
Oil on canvas 60 x 40 cm

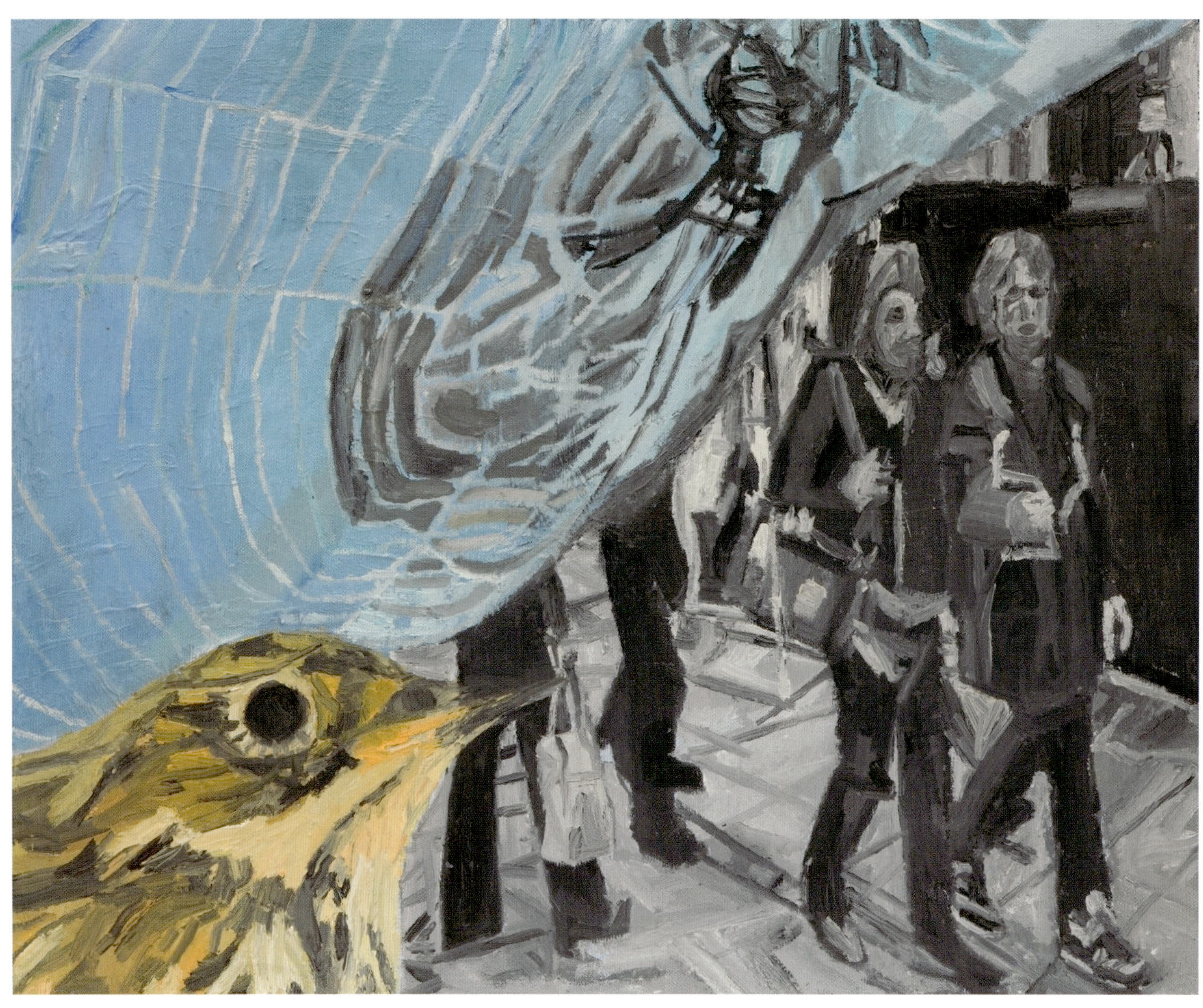

WEAVING, FLYING, WALKING 2017
Oil on canvas 60 x 40 cm

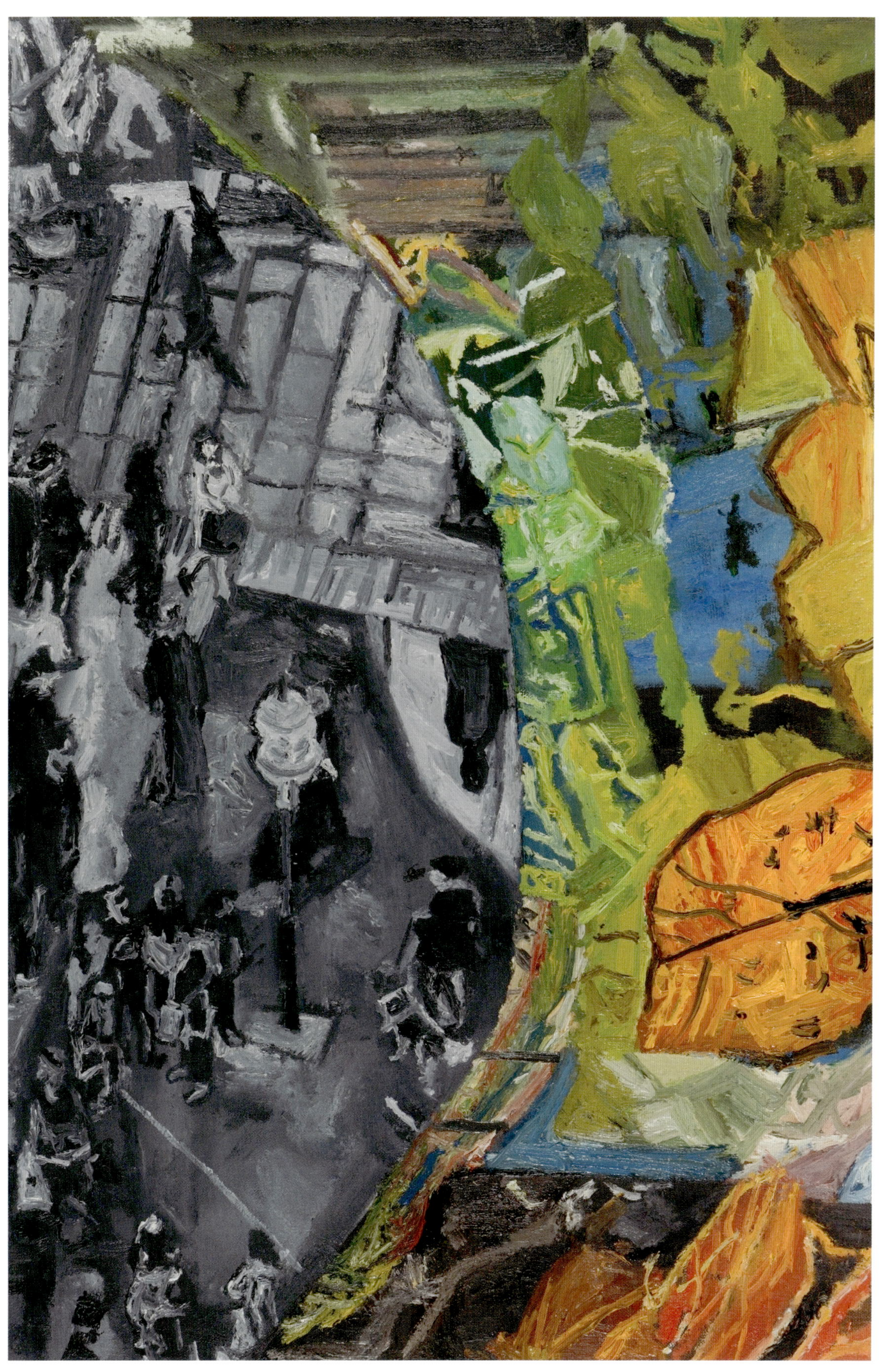

NATURBAN 2017
Oil on canvas 60 x 40 cm

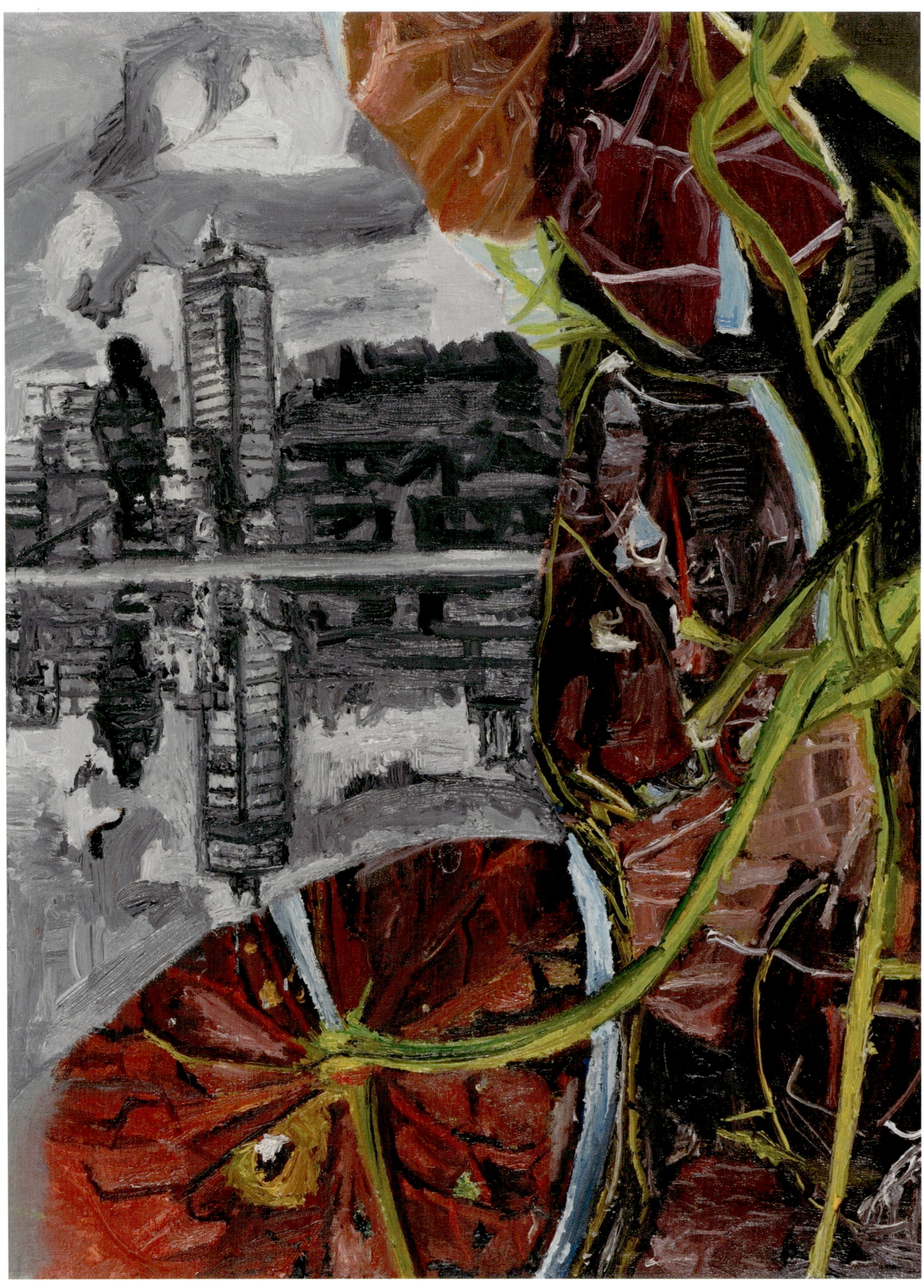

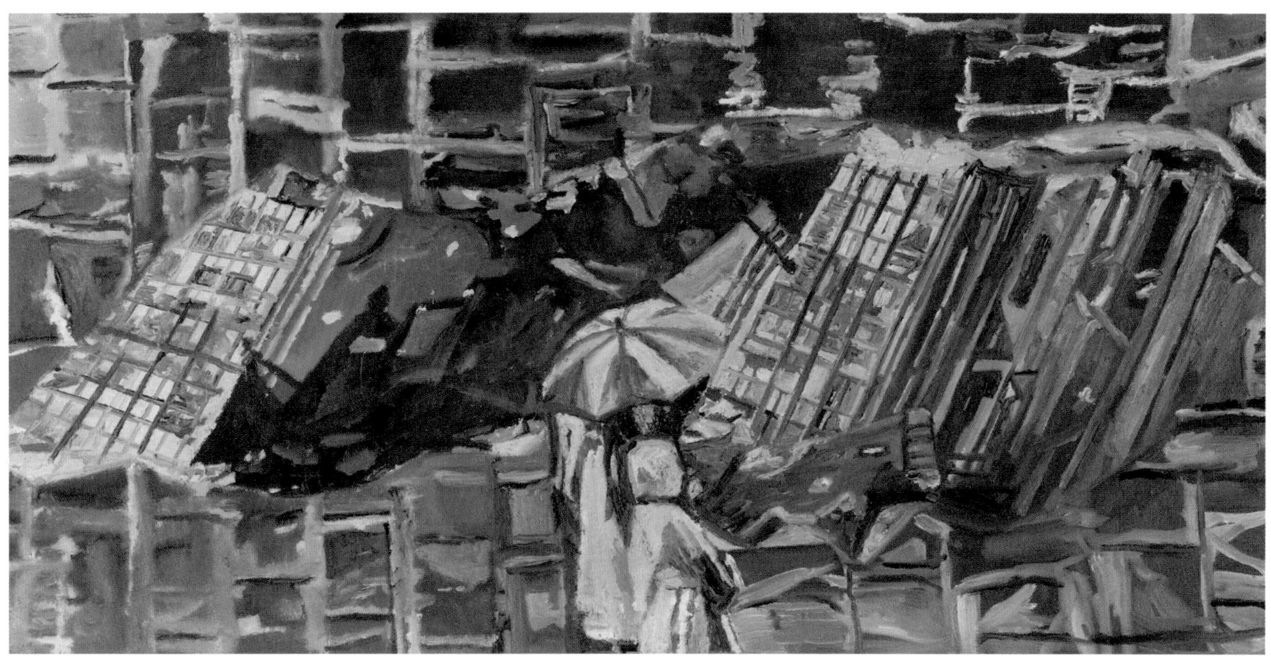

WANDERERS WALL 2017
Oil on canvas 100 x 65 cm

FAUNA MIST 2017
Oil on canvas 60 x 40 cm

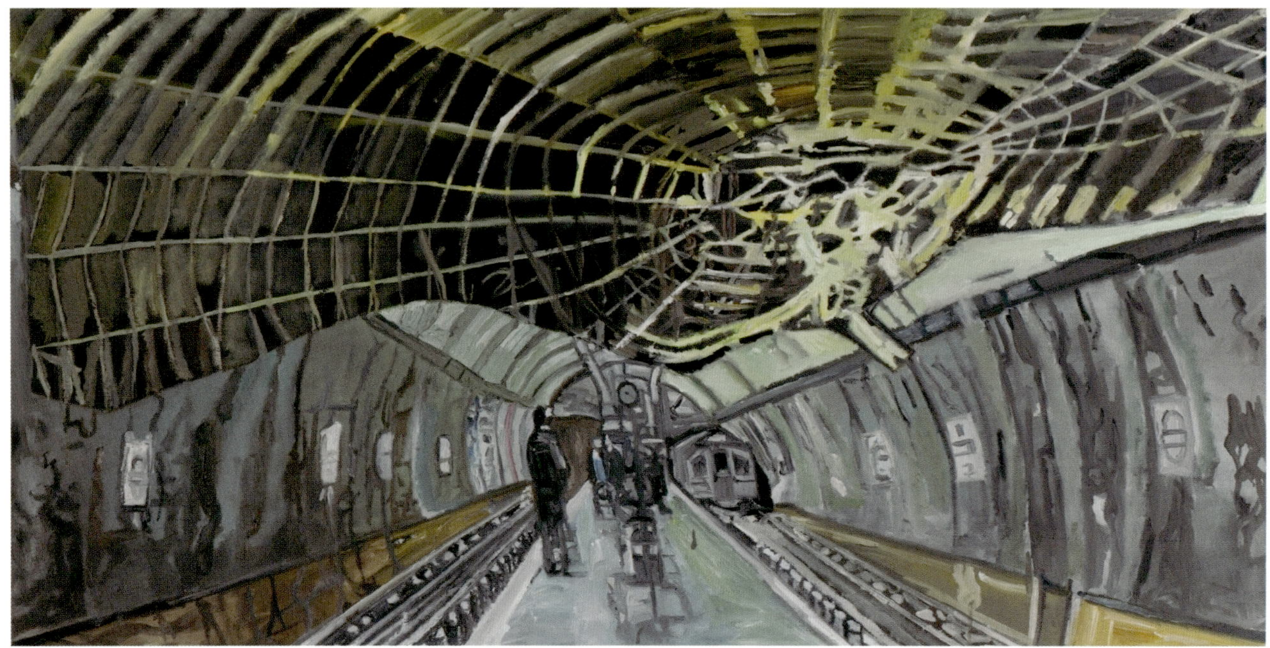

SPIRALS 2017
Oil on canvas 100 x 65 cm

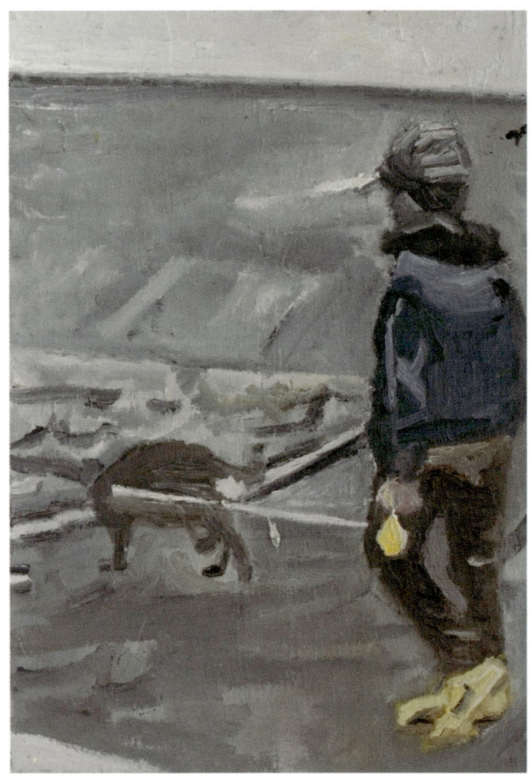

SOLITUDE 2017
Oil on canvas 35 x 24 cm

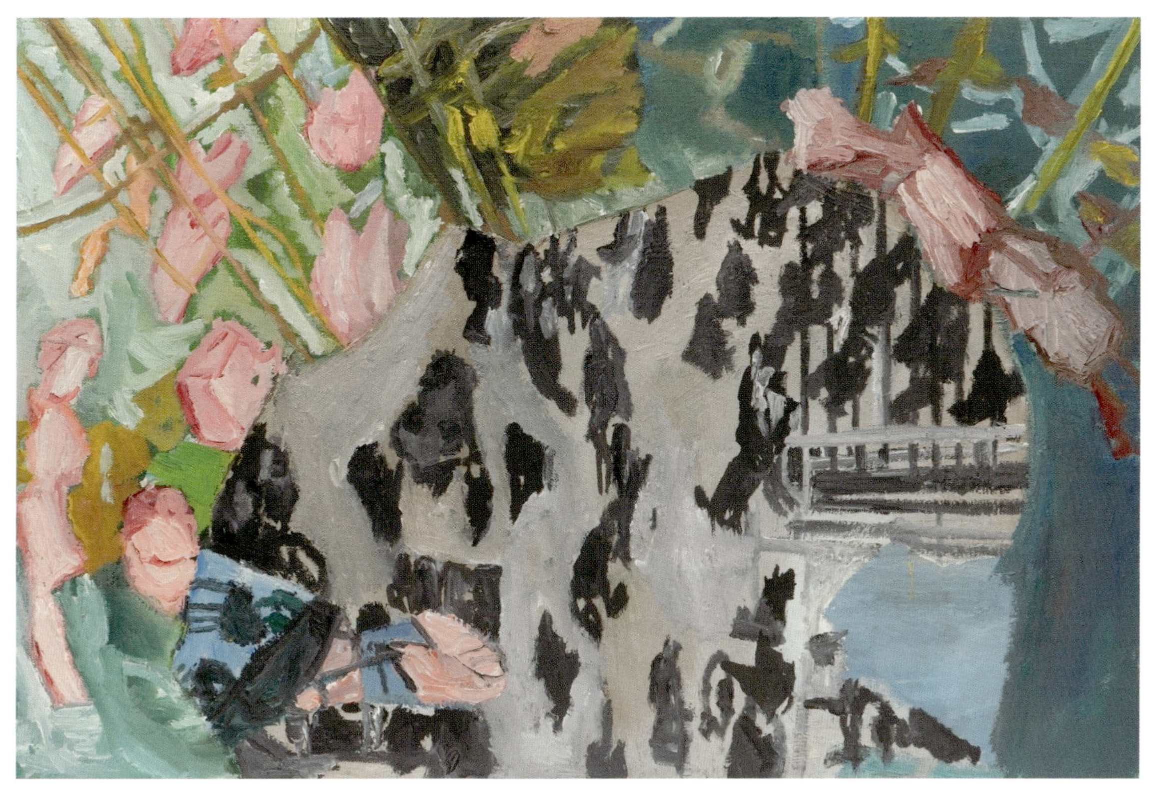

THROUGH THE FOLIAGE 2017
Oil on canvas 60 x 40 cm

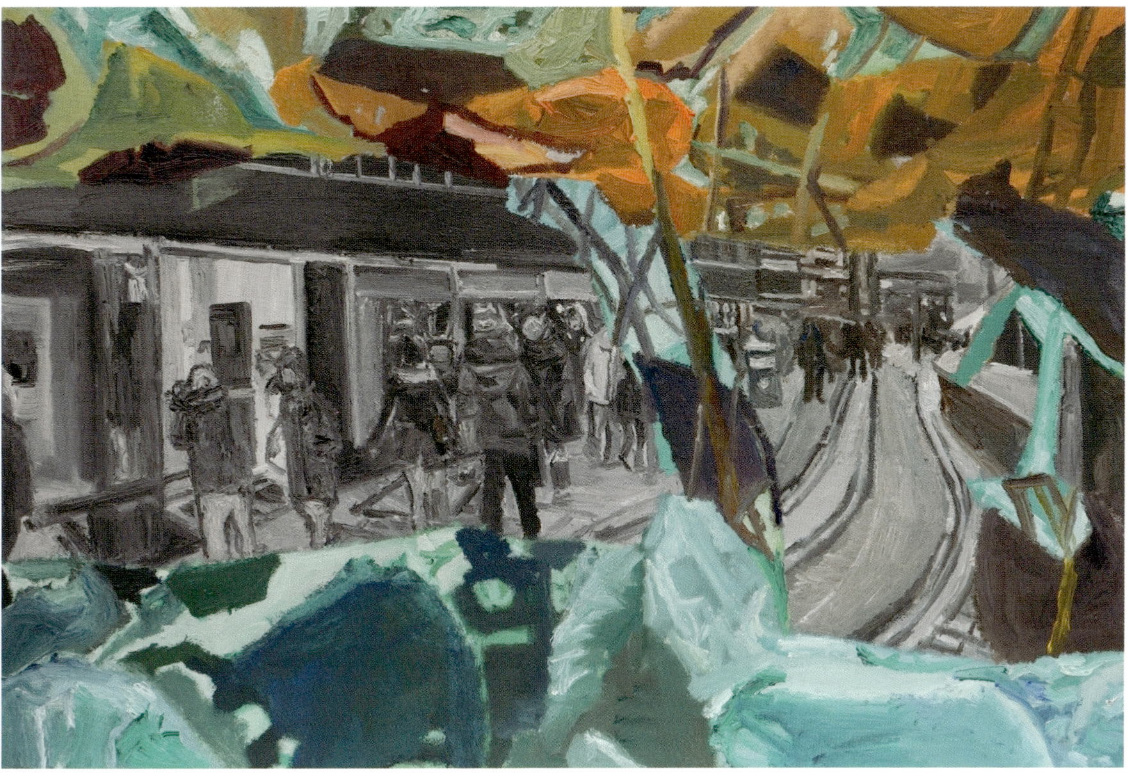

URBAN FLUX 2017
Oil on canvas 60 x 40 cm

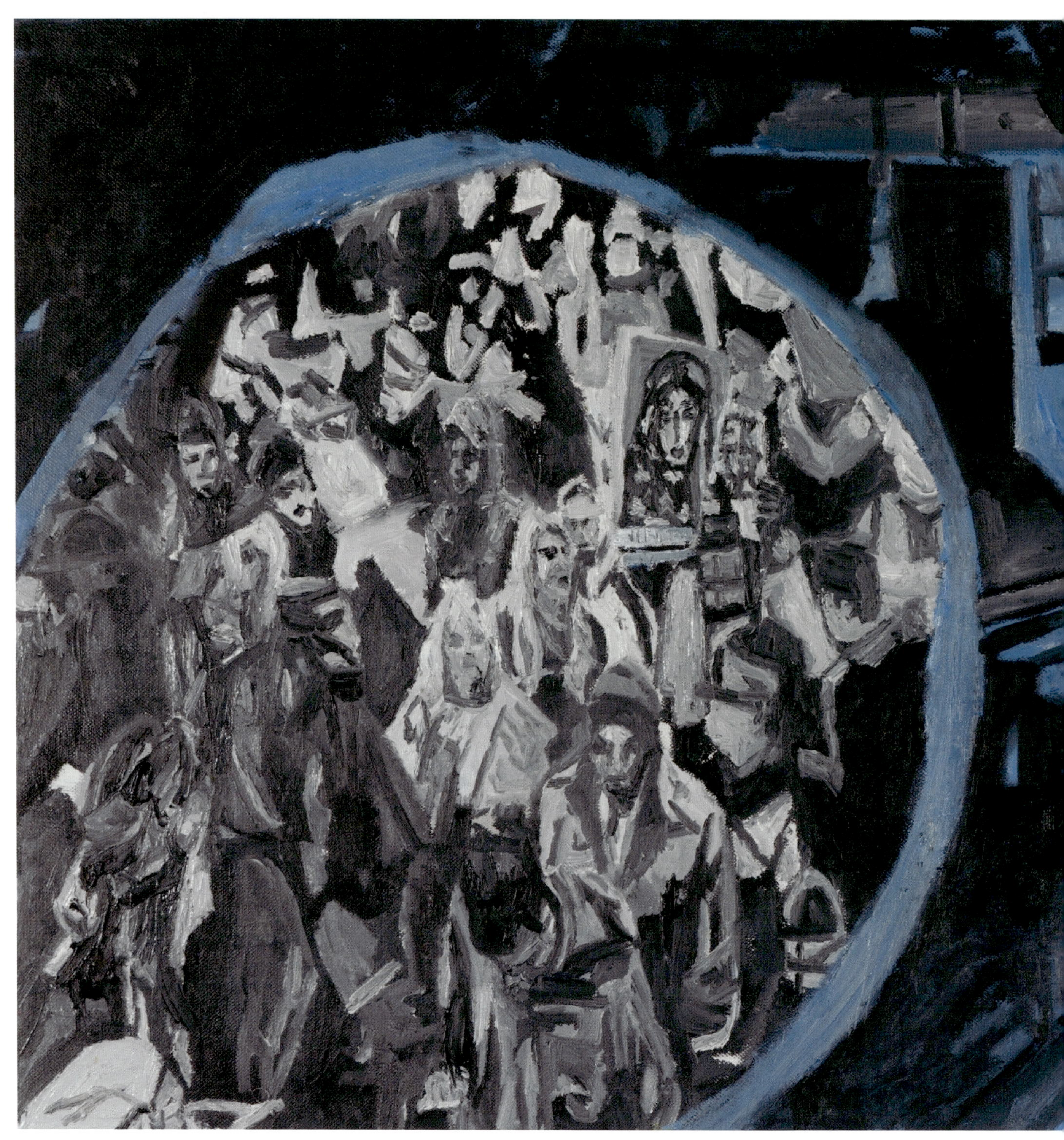

PROTEST 2017
Oil on canvas 100 x 65 cm

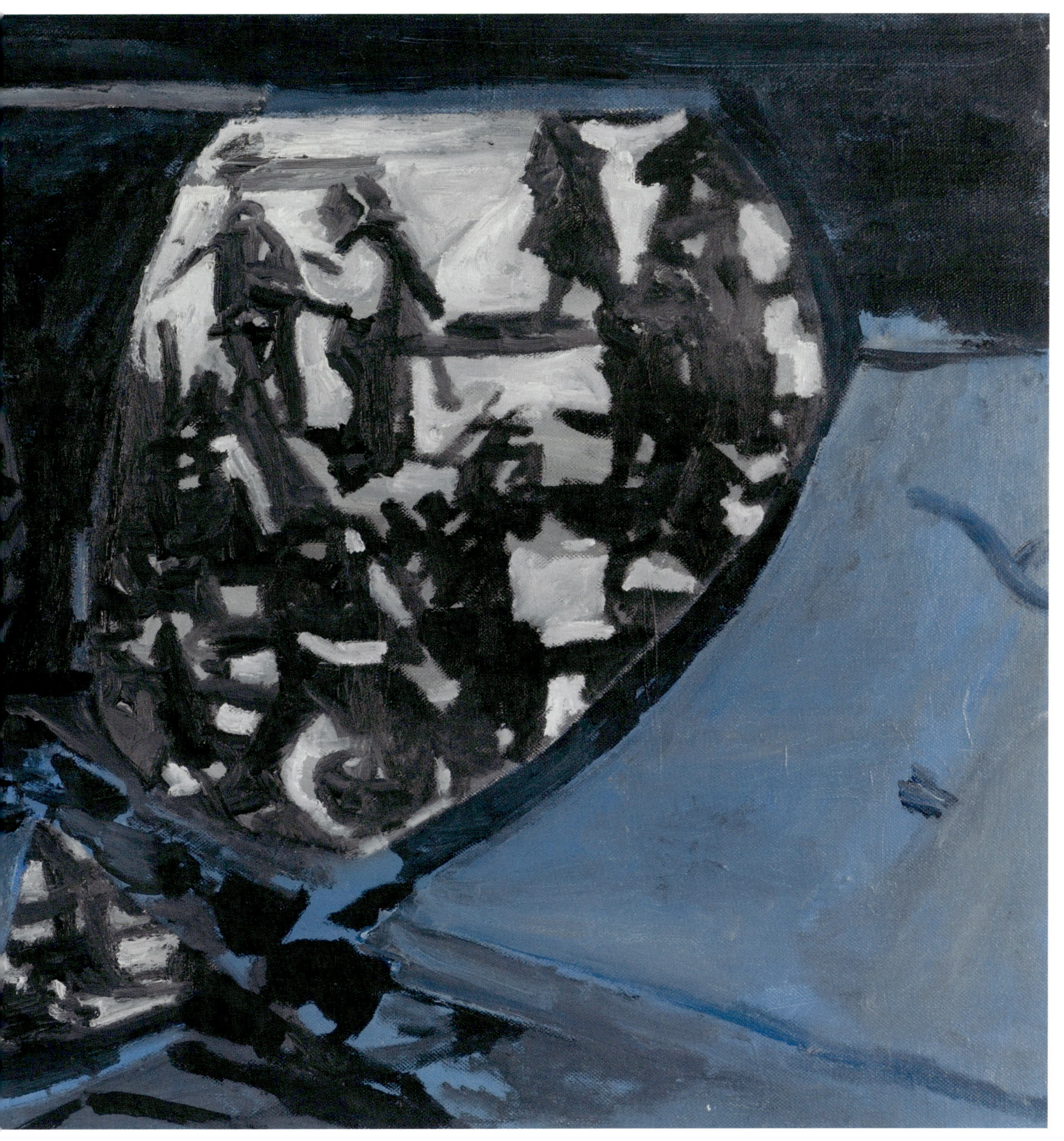

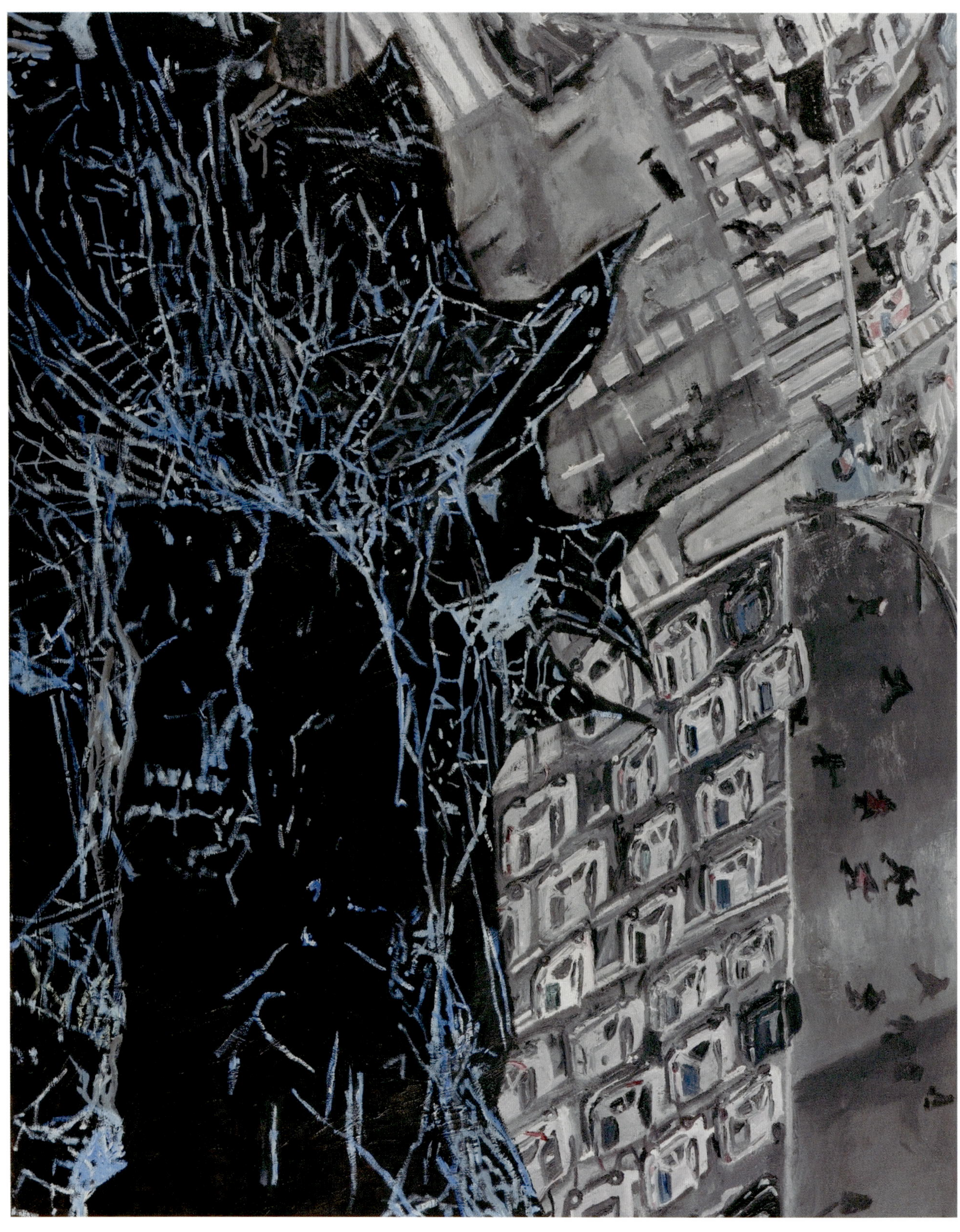

AEROTOPIA 2017
Oil on canvas 120 x 90 cm

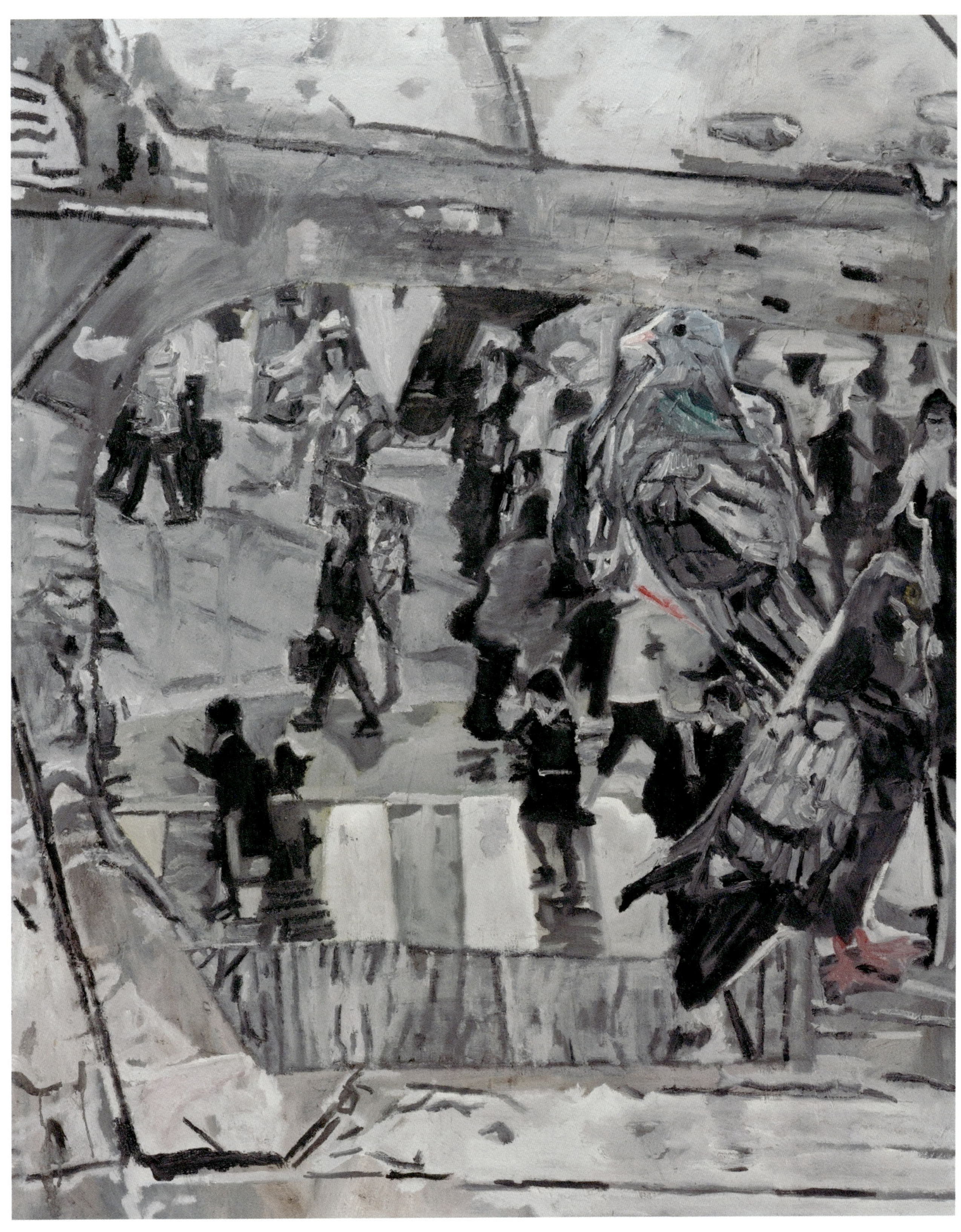

TO OBSERVE 2017
Oil on canvas 120 x 90 cm

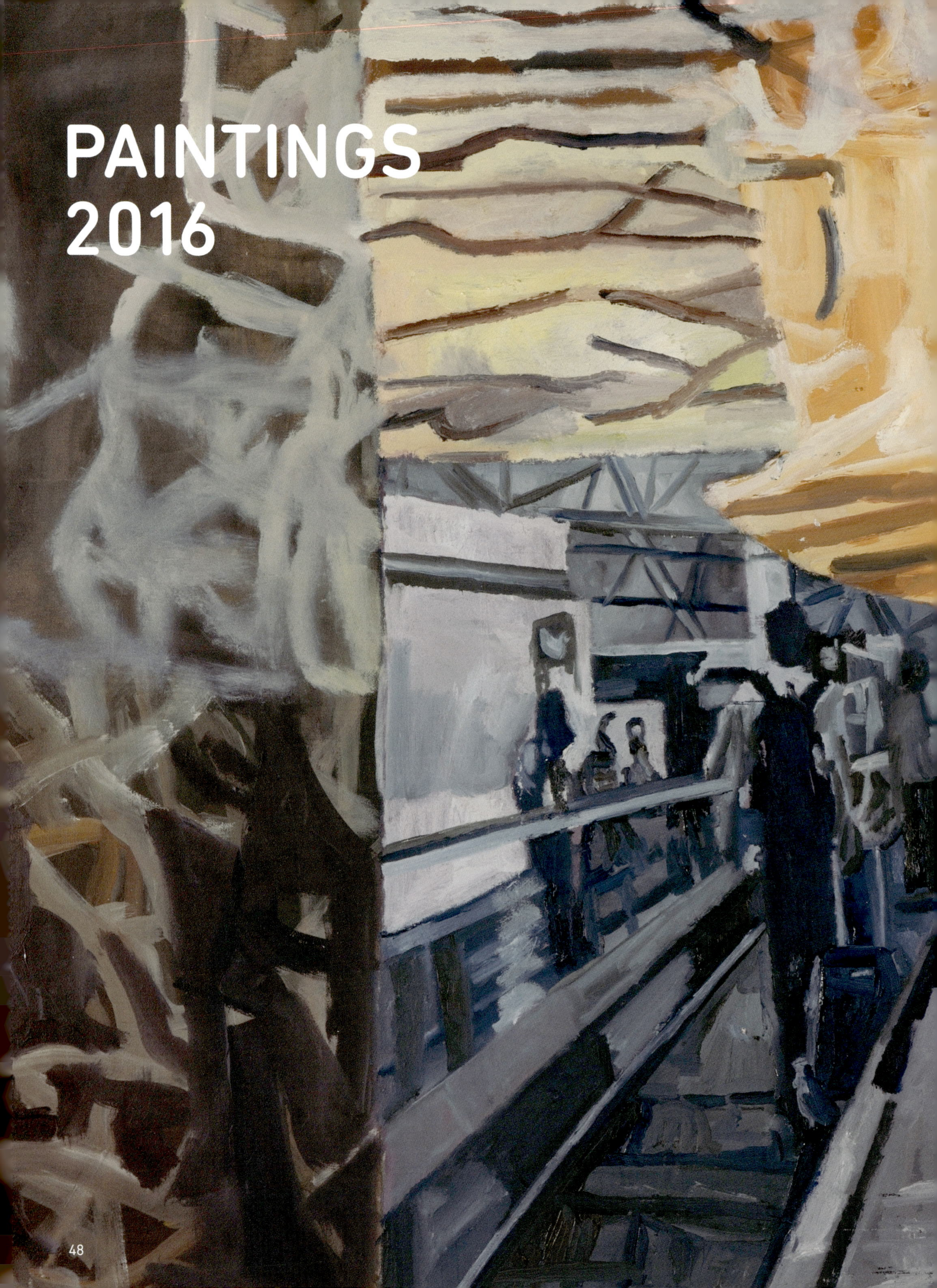
PAINTINGS
2016

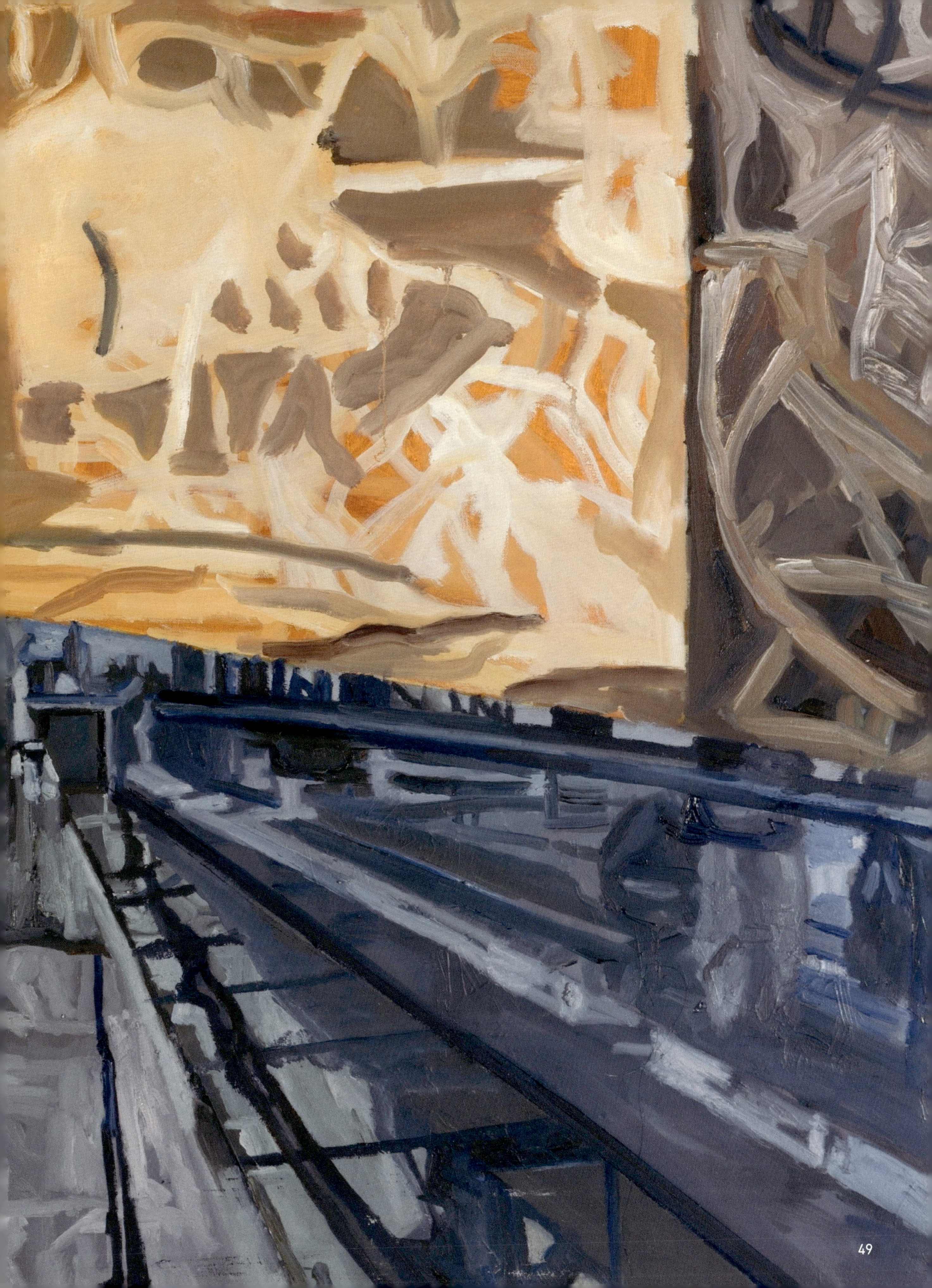

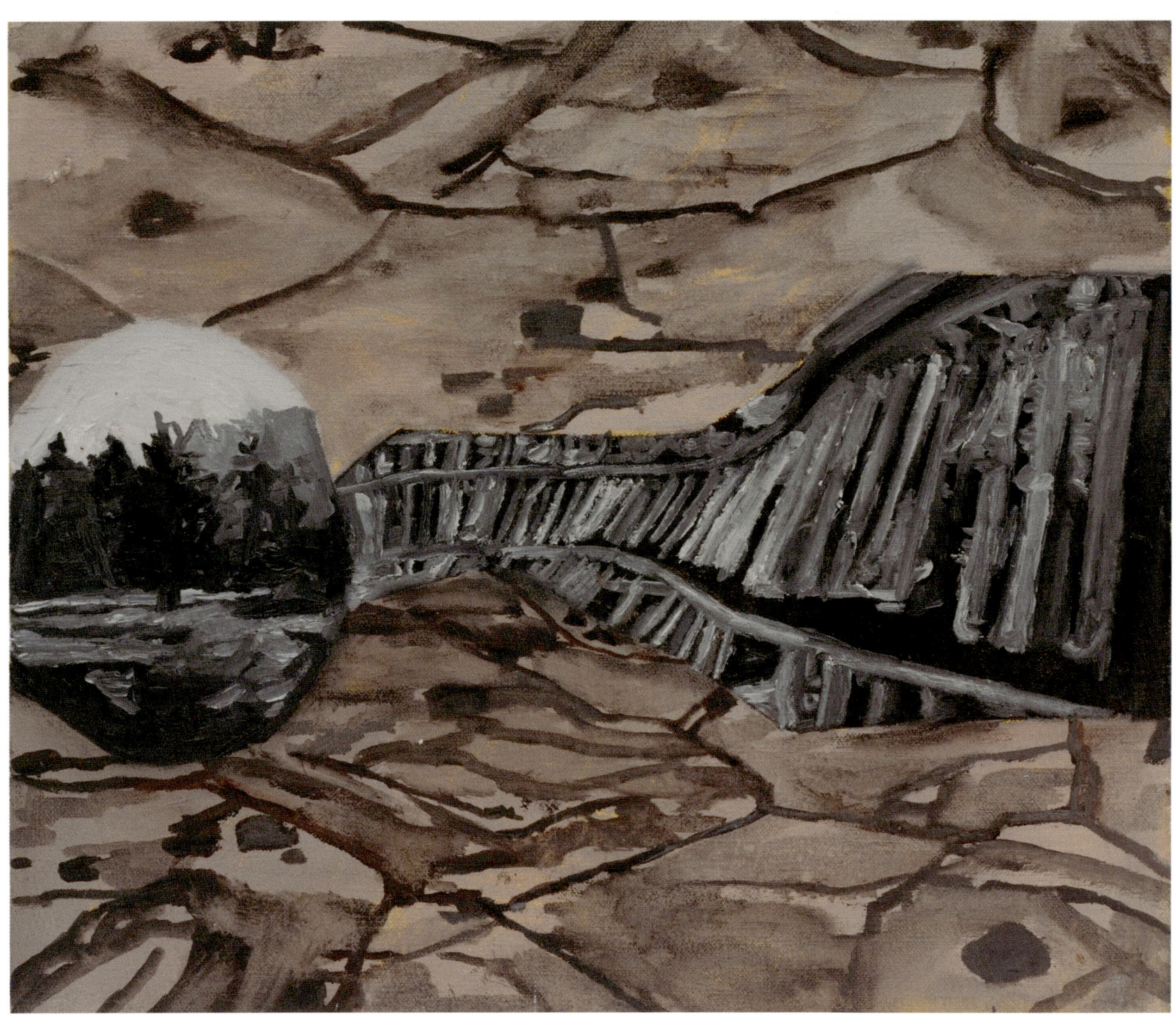

JOURNEY 2016
Oil on canvas 30 x 29 cm

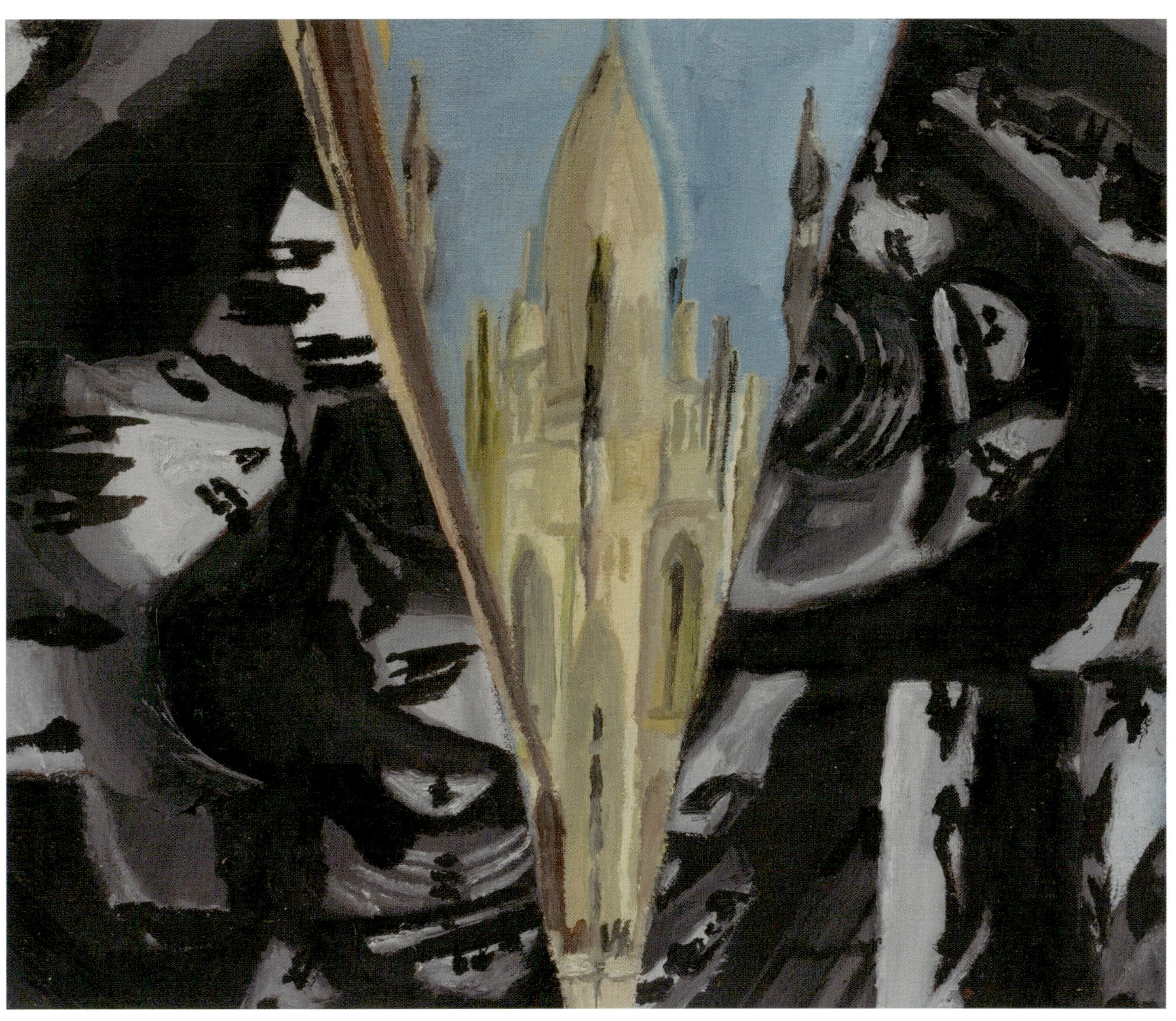

REFLECTIONS 2016
Oil on canvas 30 x 29 cm

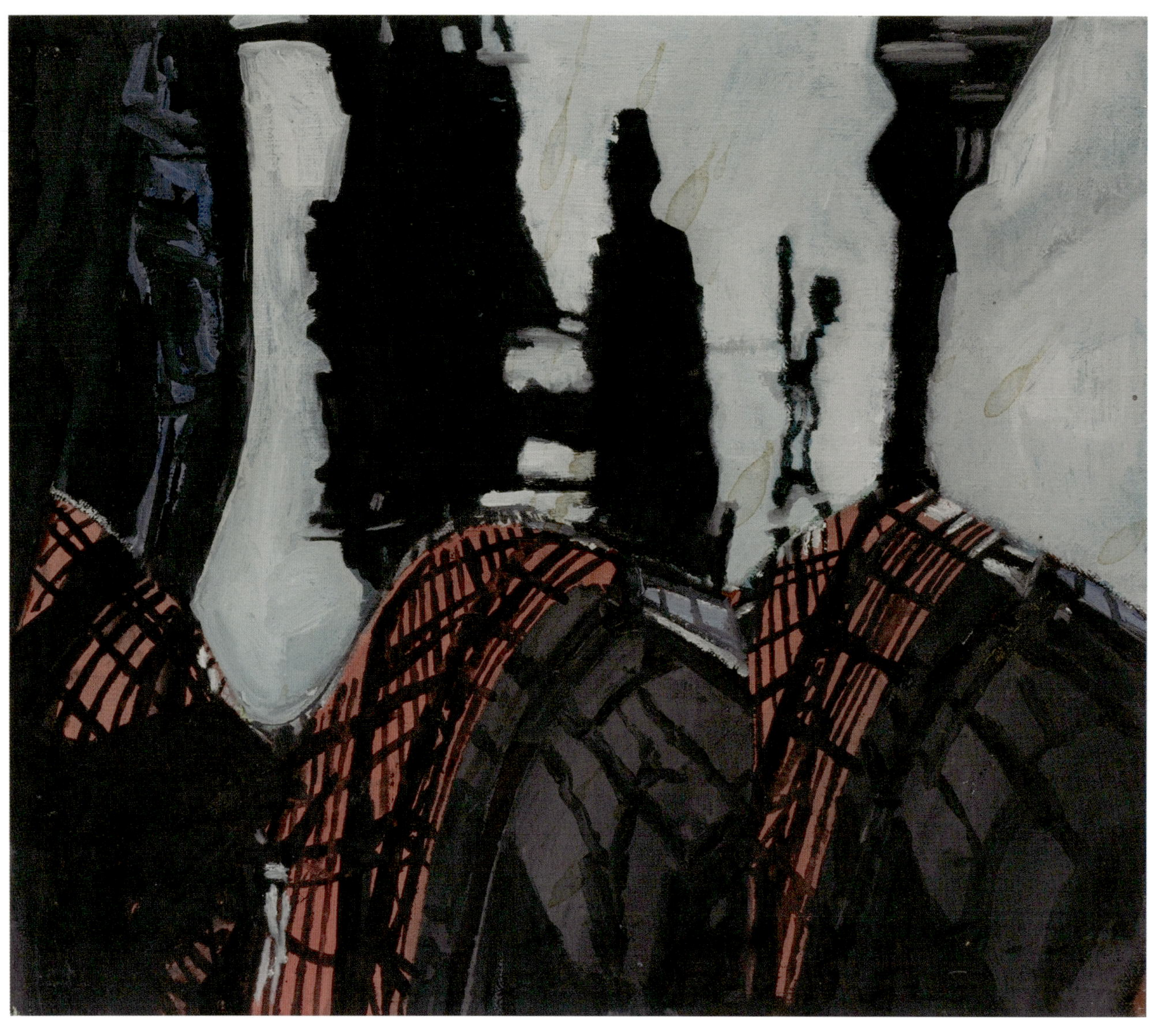

OUR PLACE 2016
Oil on canvas 30 x 29 cm

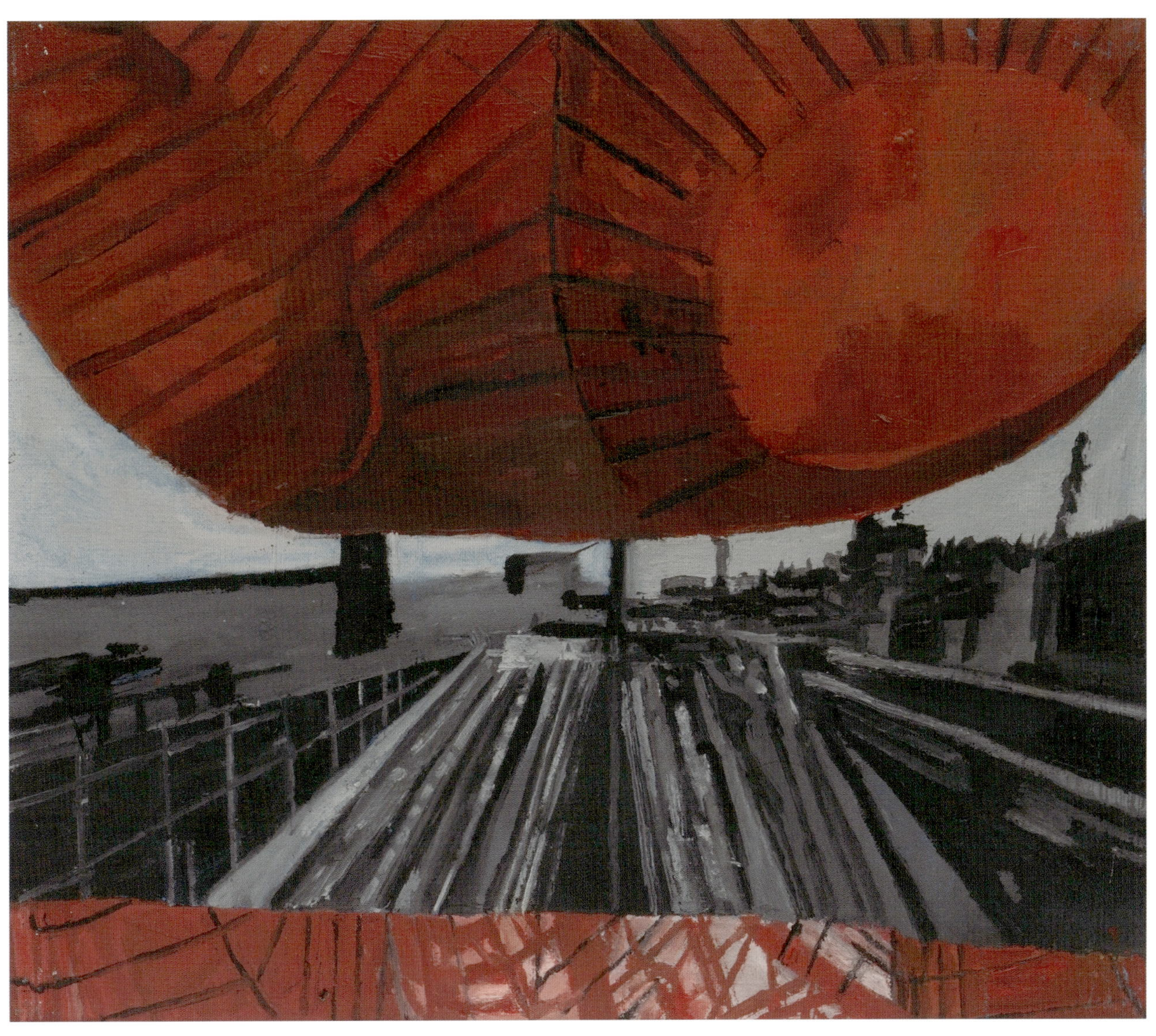

NEBULOUS 2016
Oil on canvas 30 x 29 cm

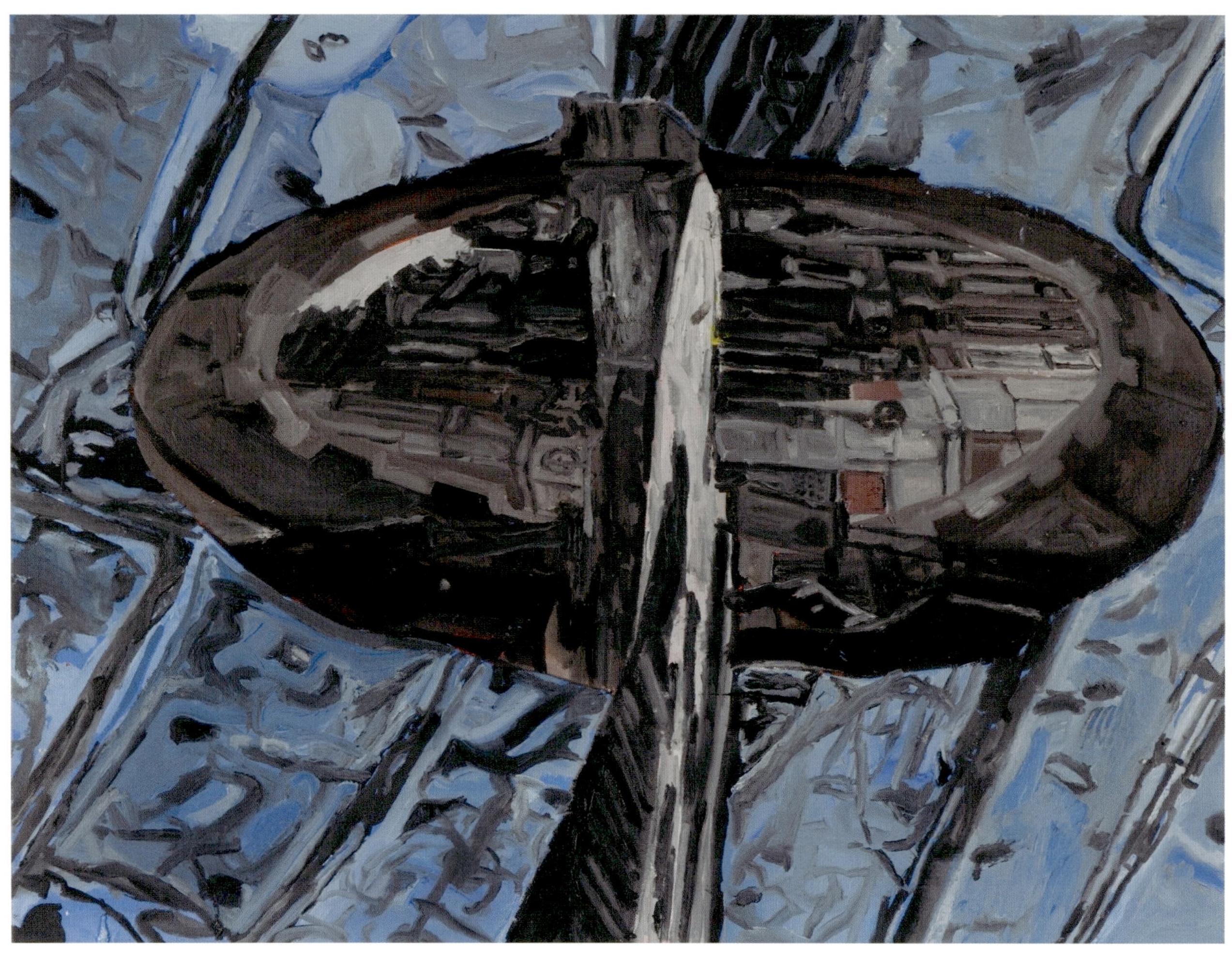

ON THE EDGE 2016
Oil canvas 90 x 60 cm

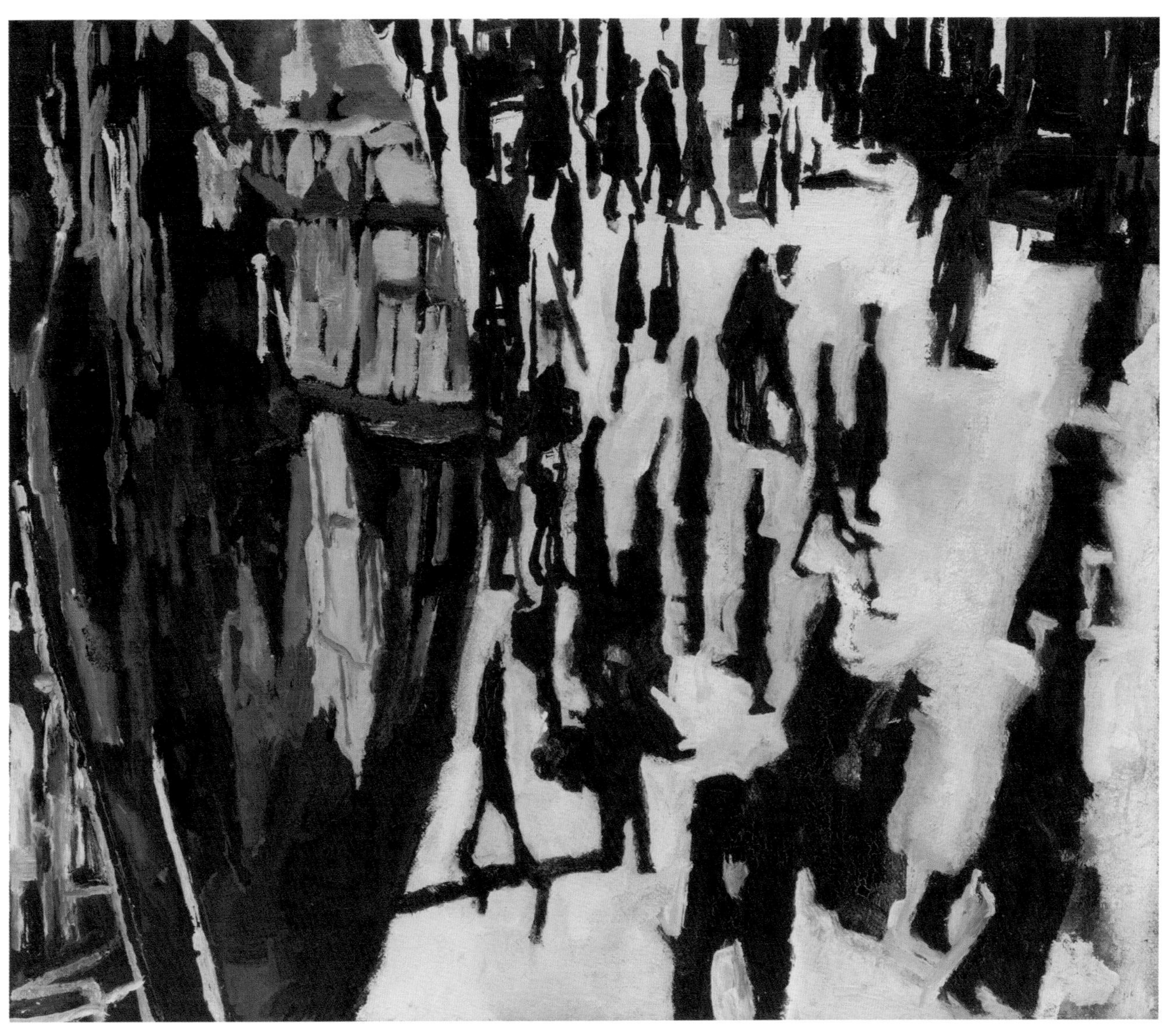

WANDERERS 2016
Oil on canvas 30 x 29 cm

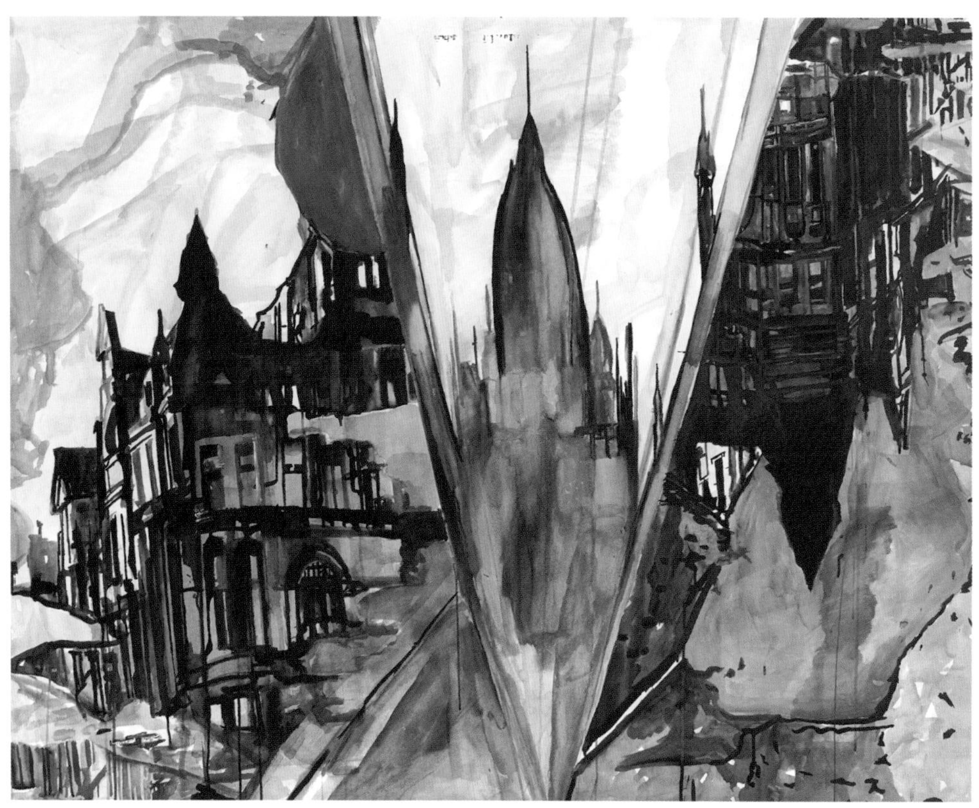

SHADOW 2016
Ink on paper 150 x 120 cm

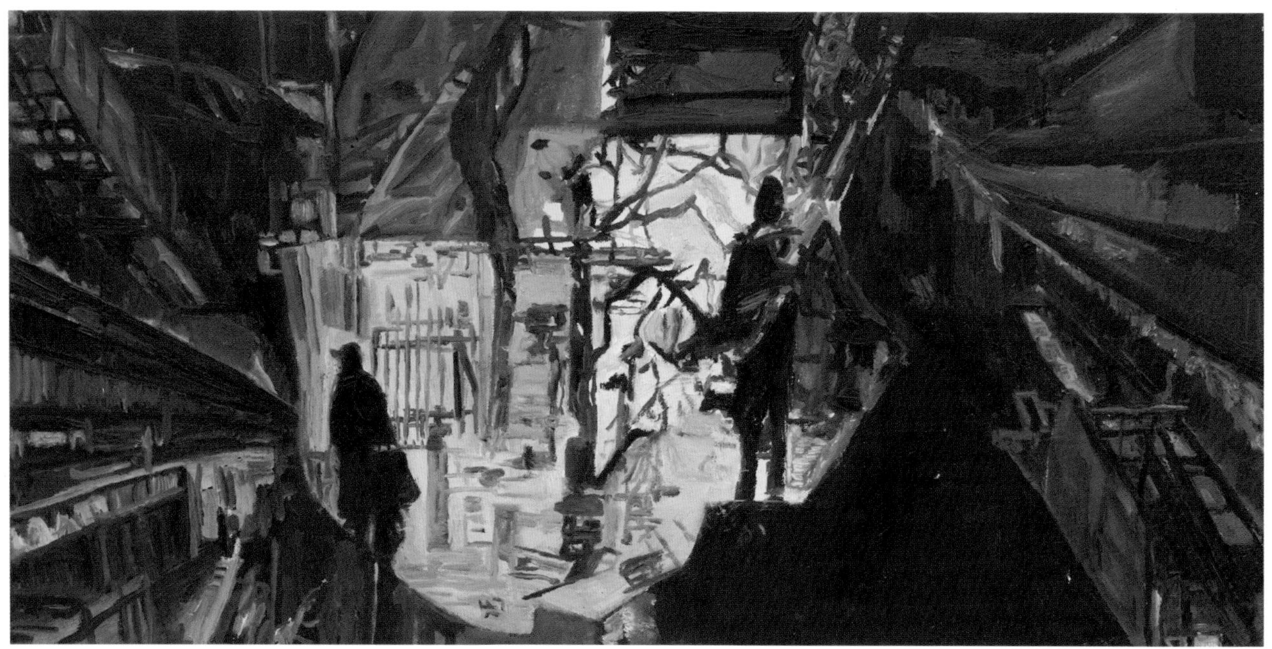

CREVICE 2016
Oil on canvas 70 x 30 cm

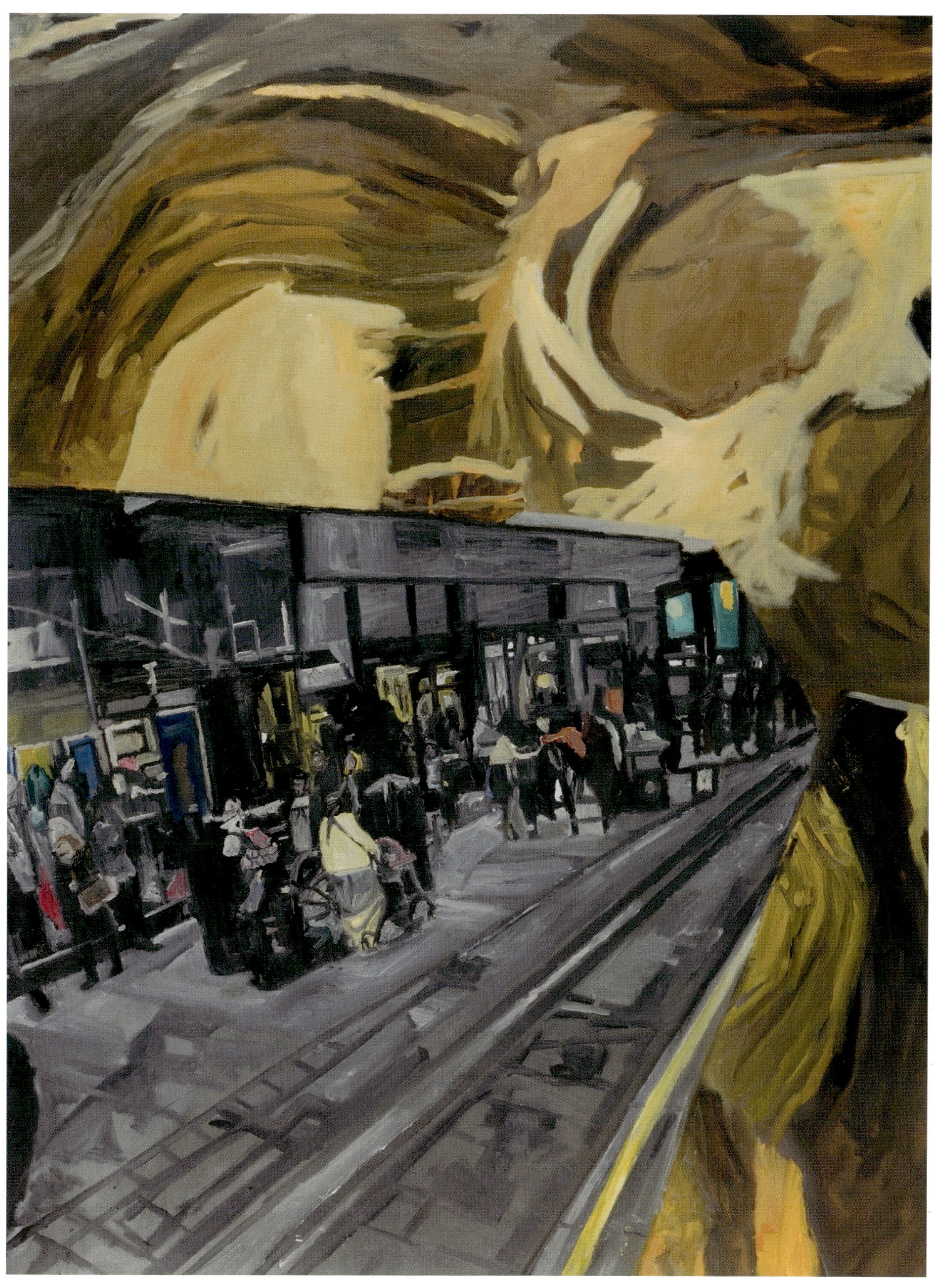

UNHEARD VOICES 2016–17
Oil on canvas 120 x 90 cm

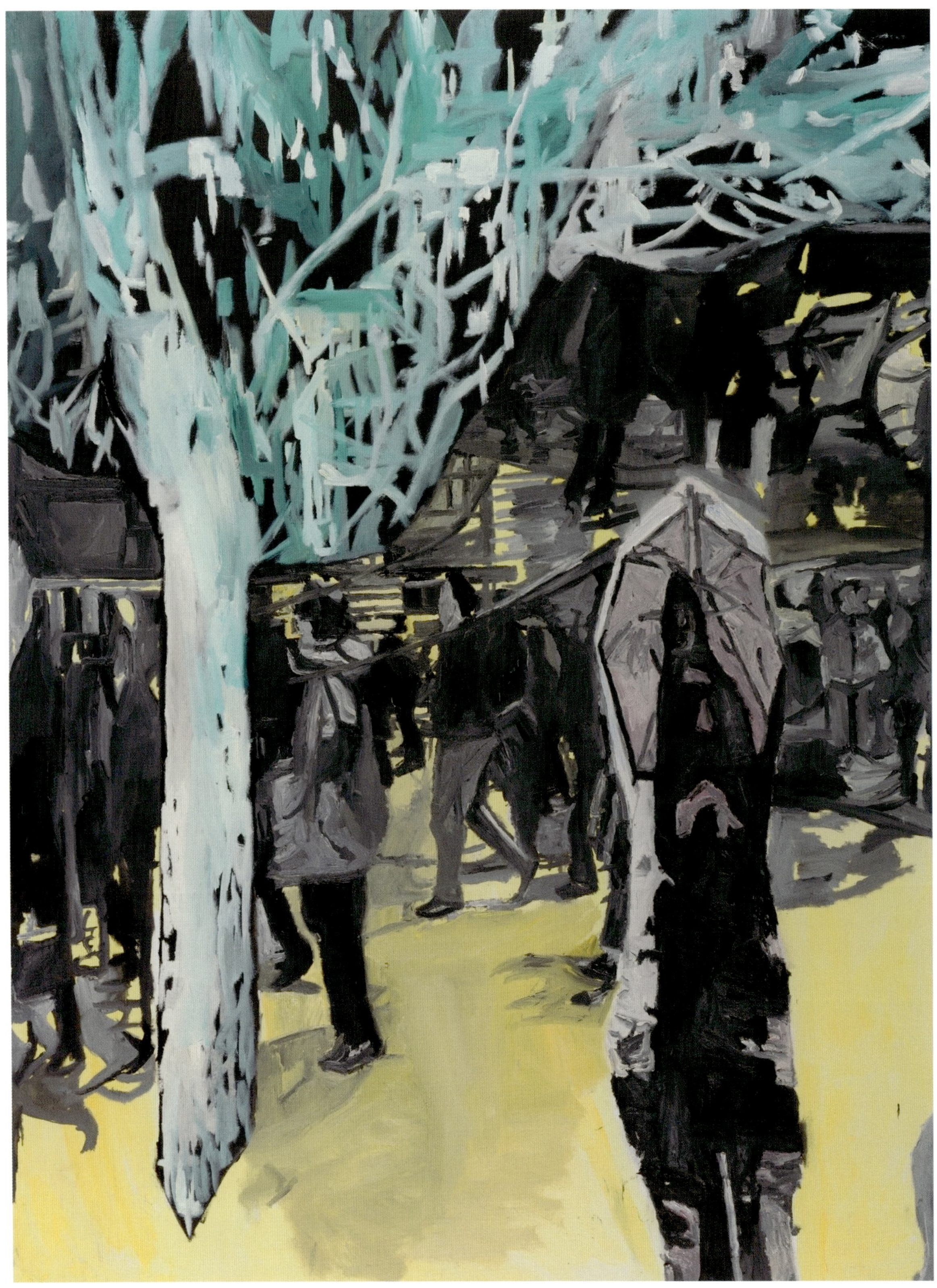

CITY WALKER 2016
Oil on canvas 120 x 90 cm

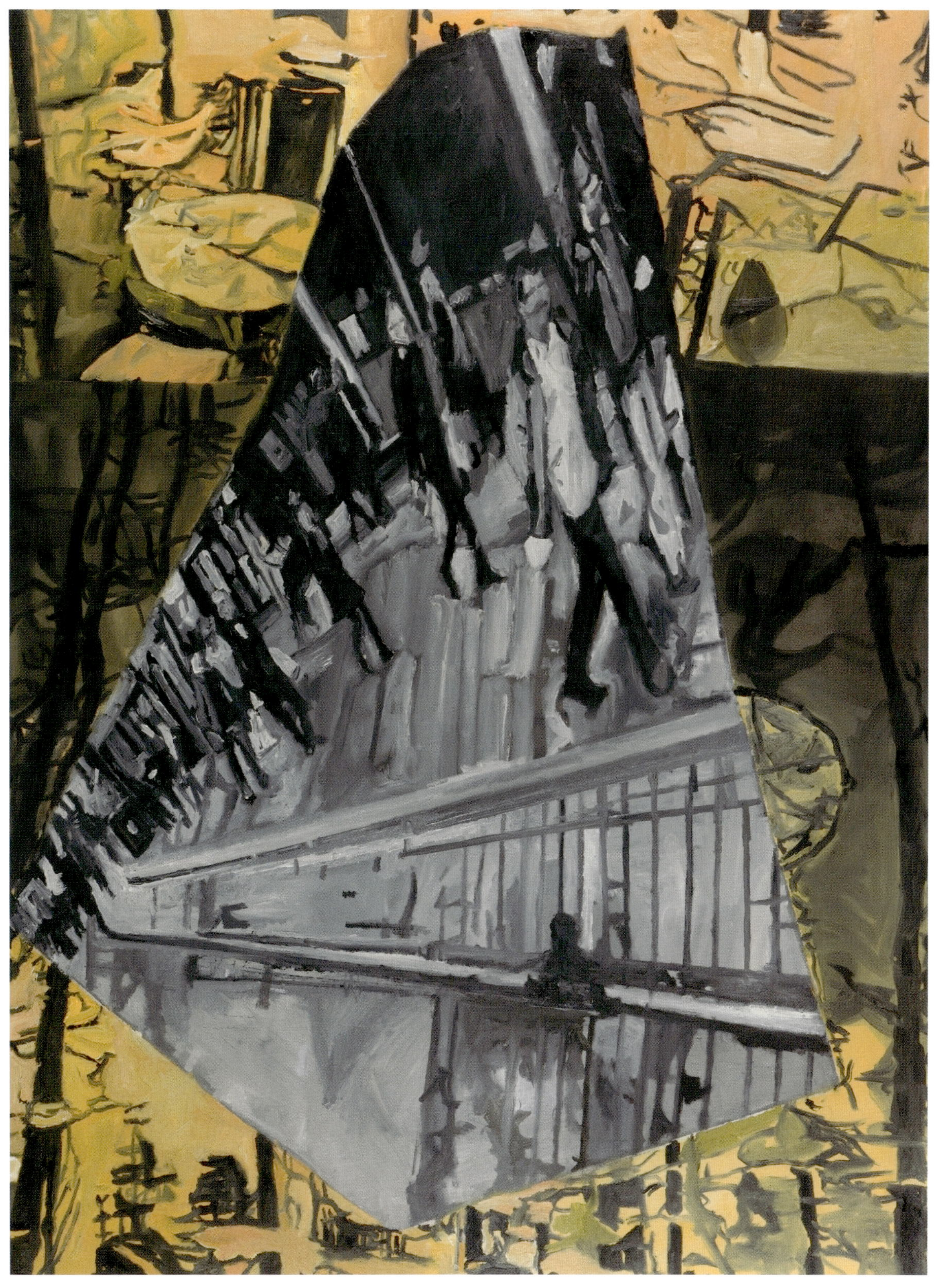

SWARM 2016
Oil on canvas 120 x 90 cm

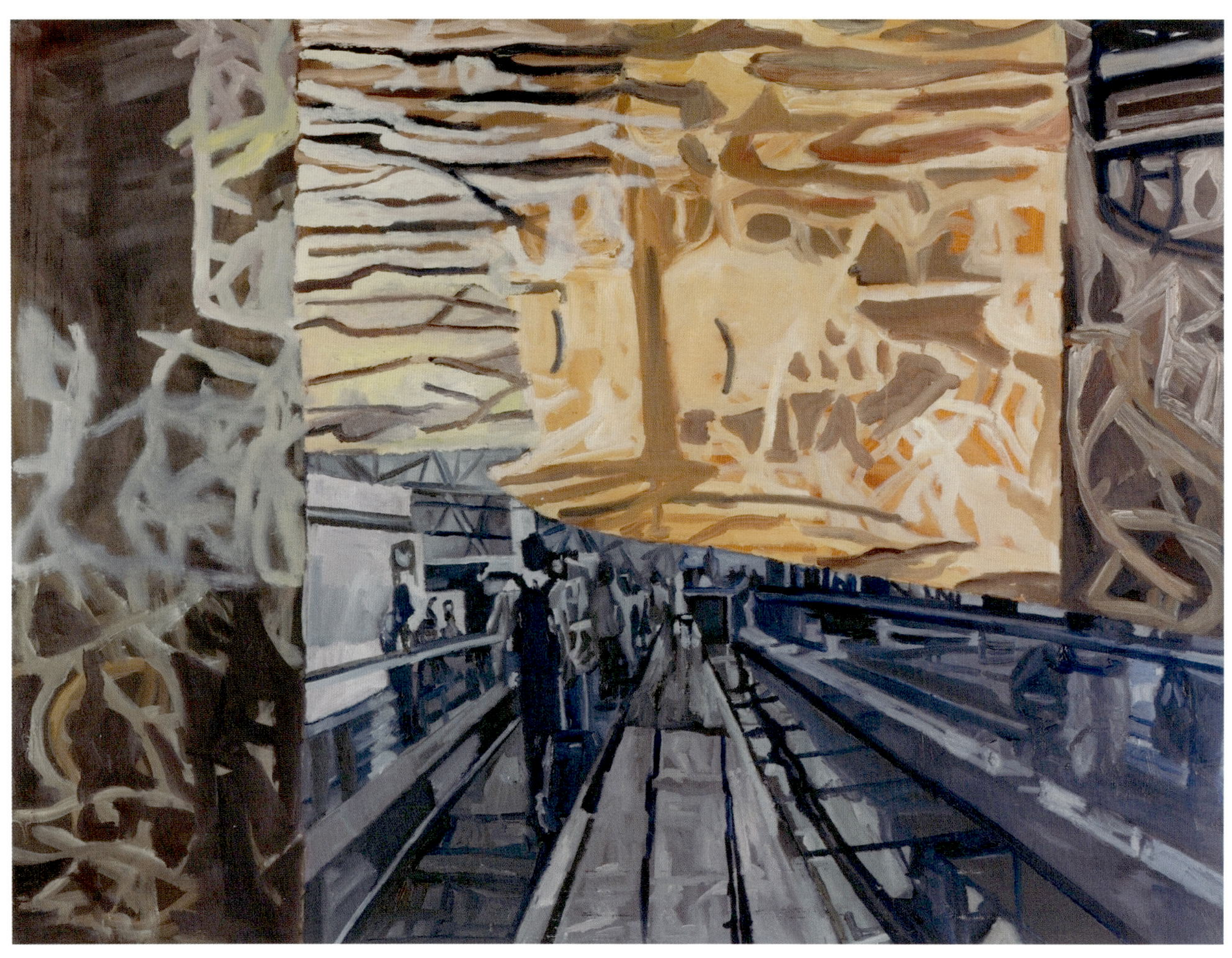

FLOOD 2016
Oil on canvas 120 x 90 cm

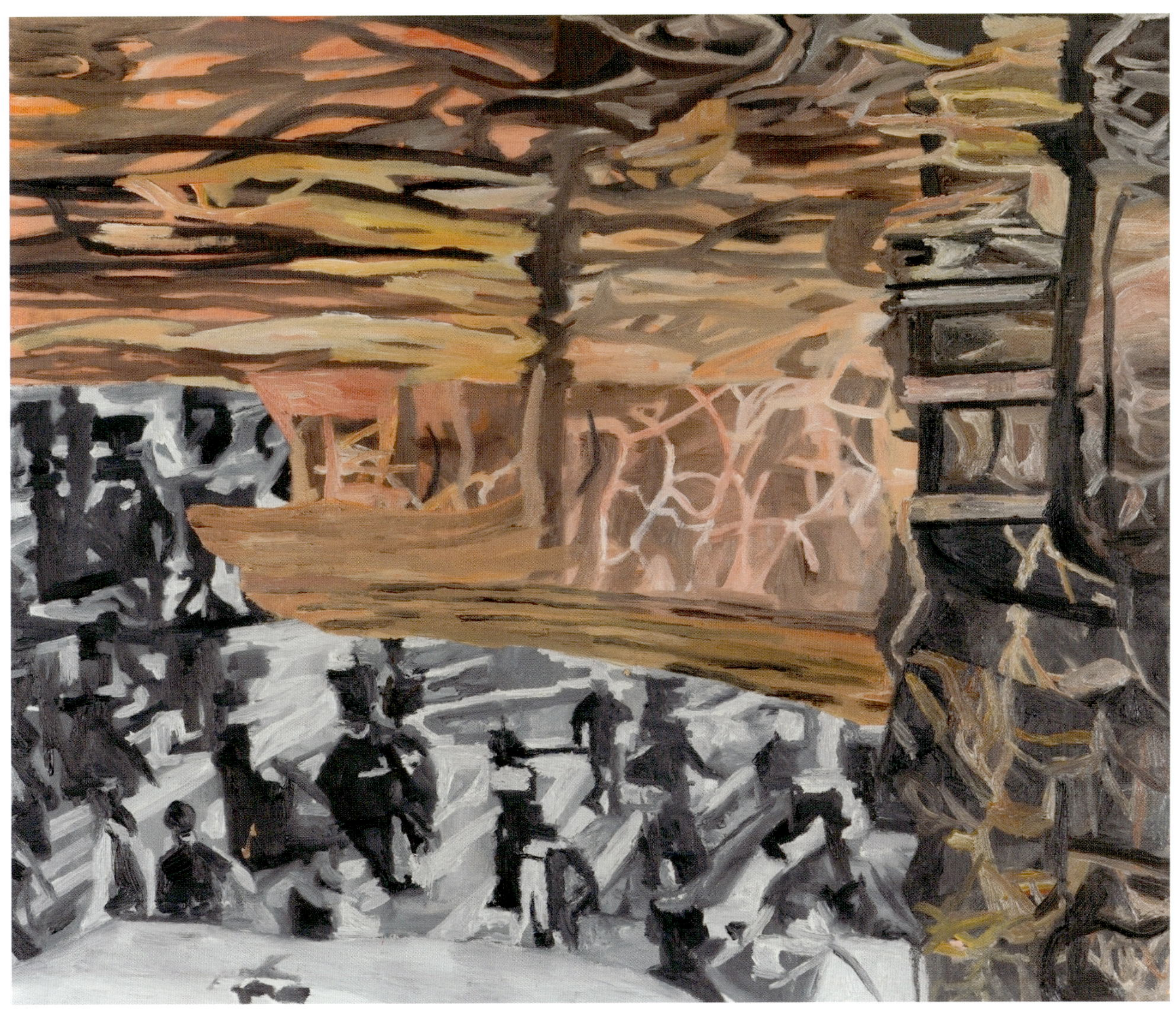

FLOOD 2016
Oil on canvas 150 x 120 cm

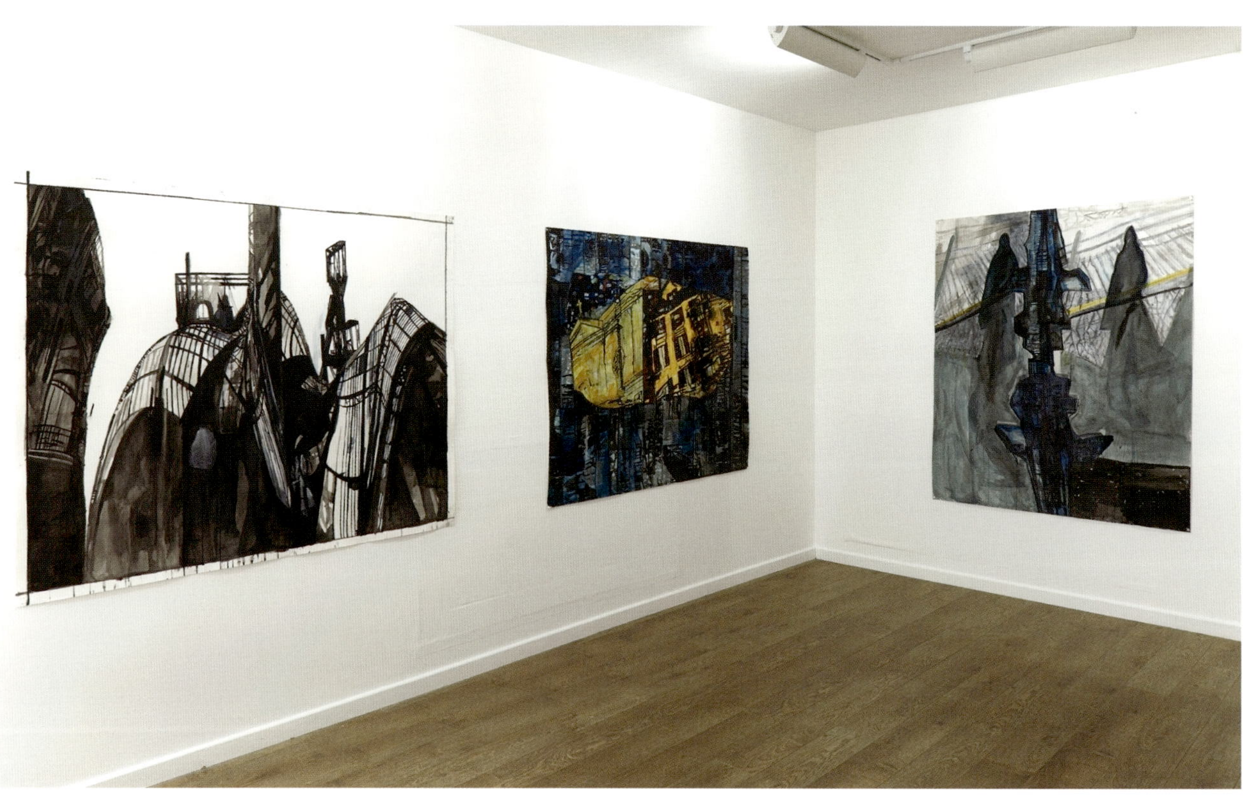

Urban Forest, solo exhibition at Delta House Studios, London 2017

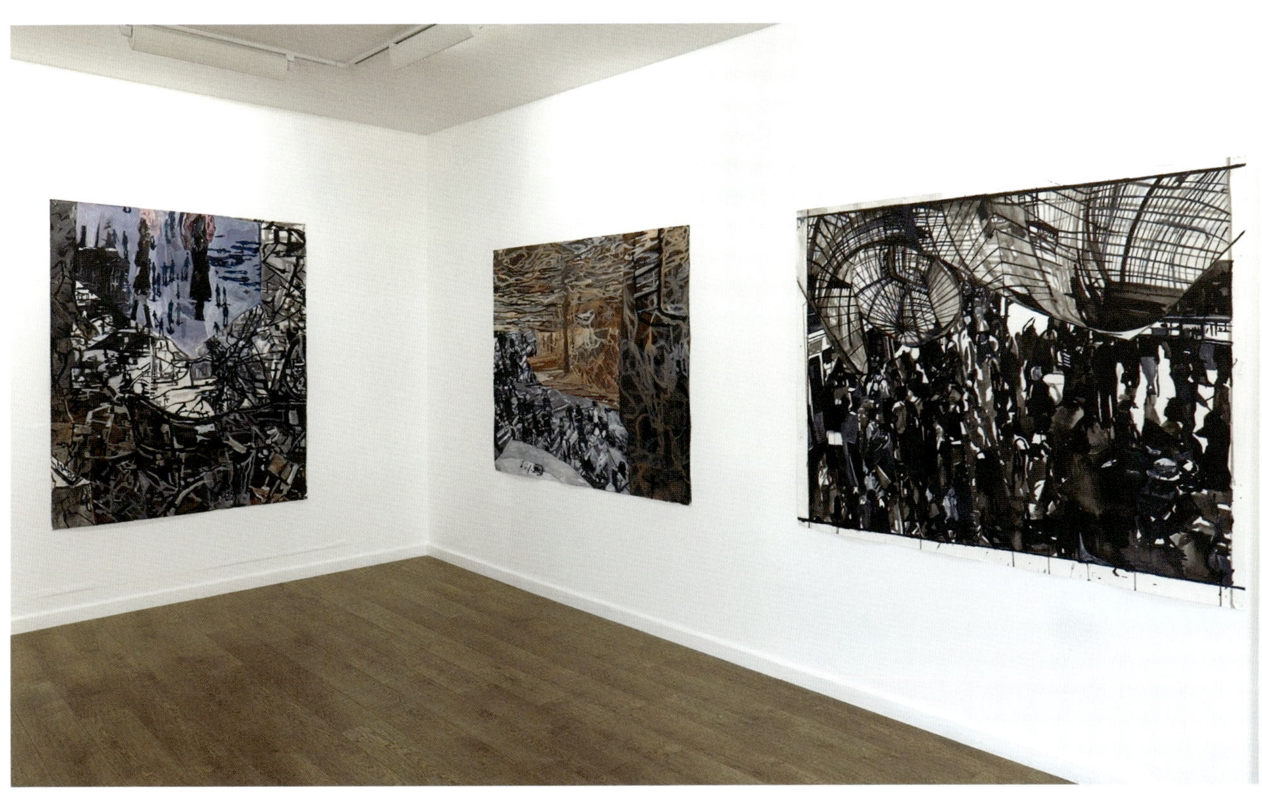

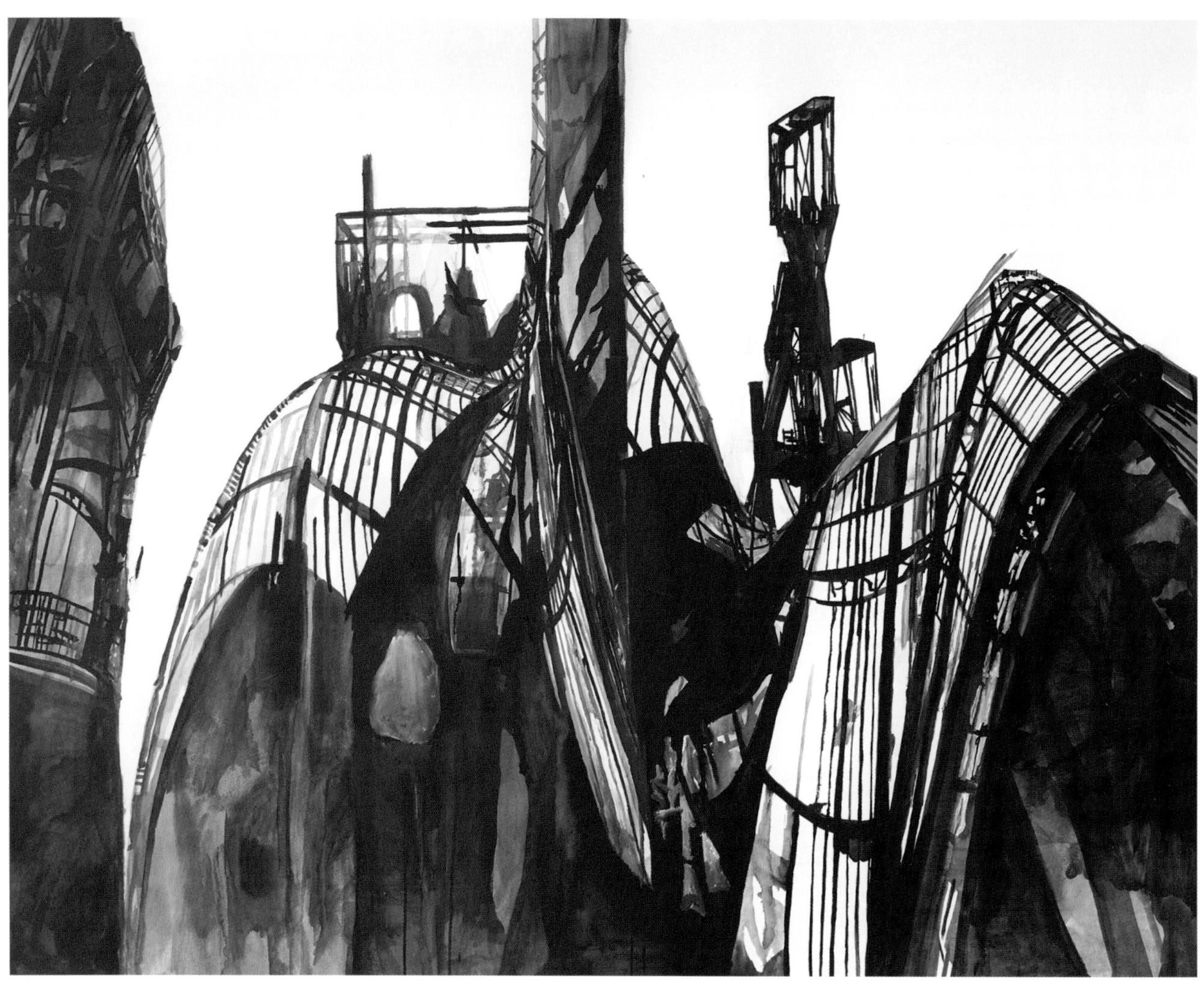

FLOW 2016
Ink on paper 150 x 120 cm

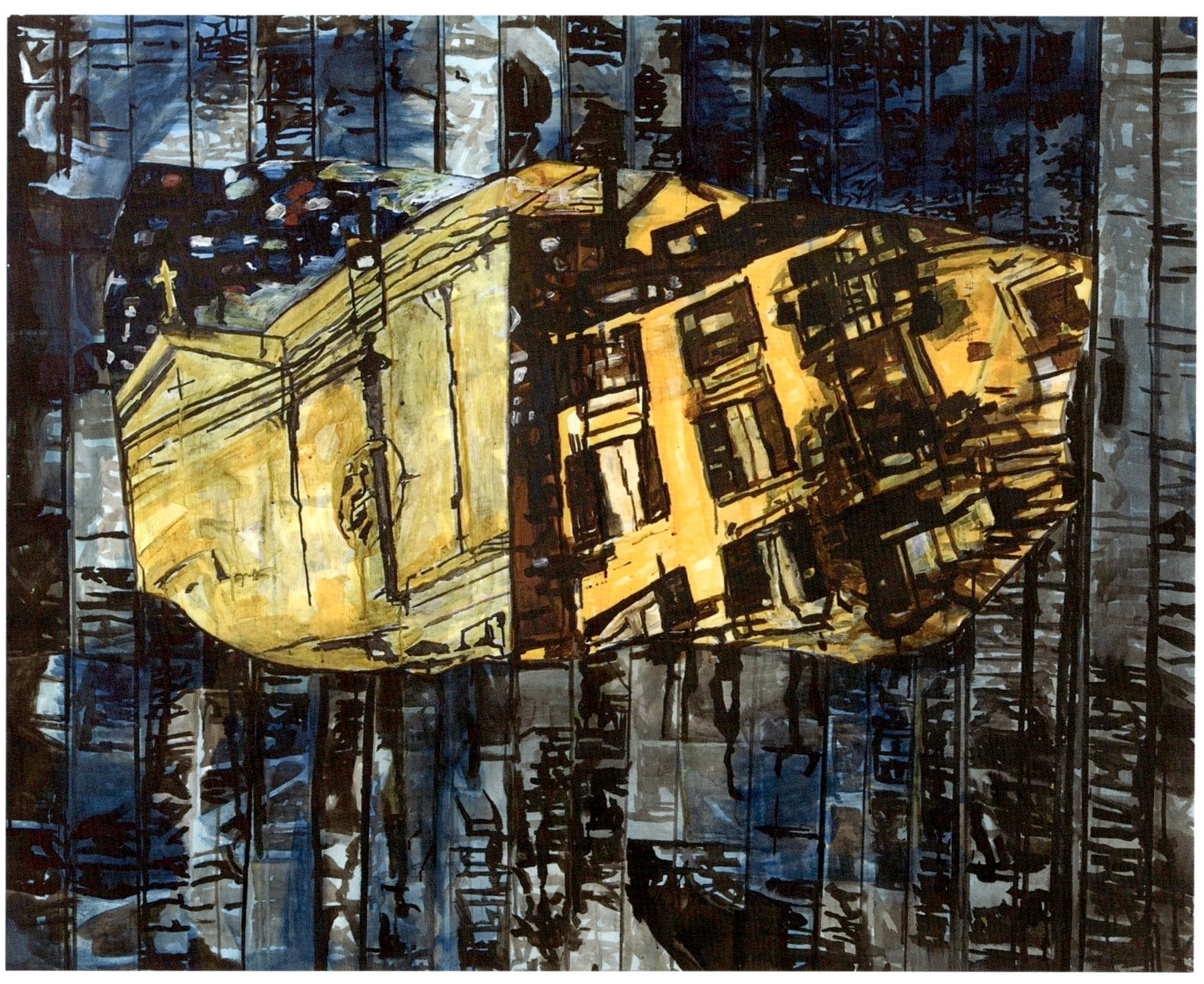

ENTRANCEMENT 2016
Ink on paper 150 x 120 cm

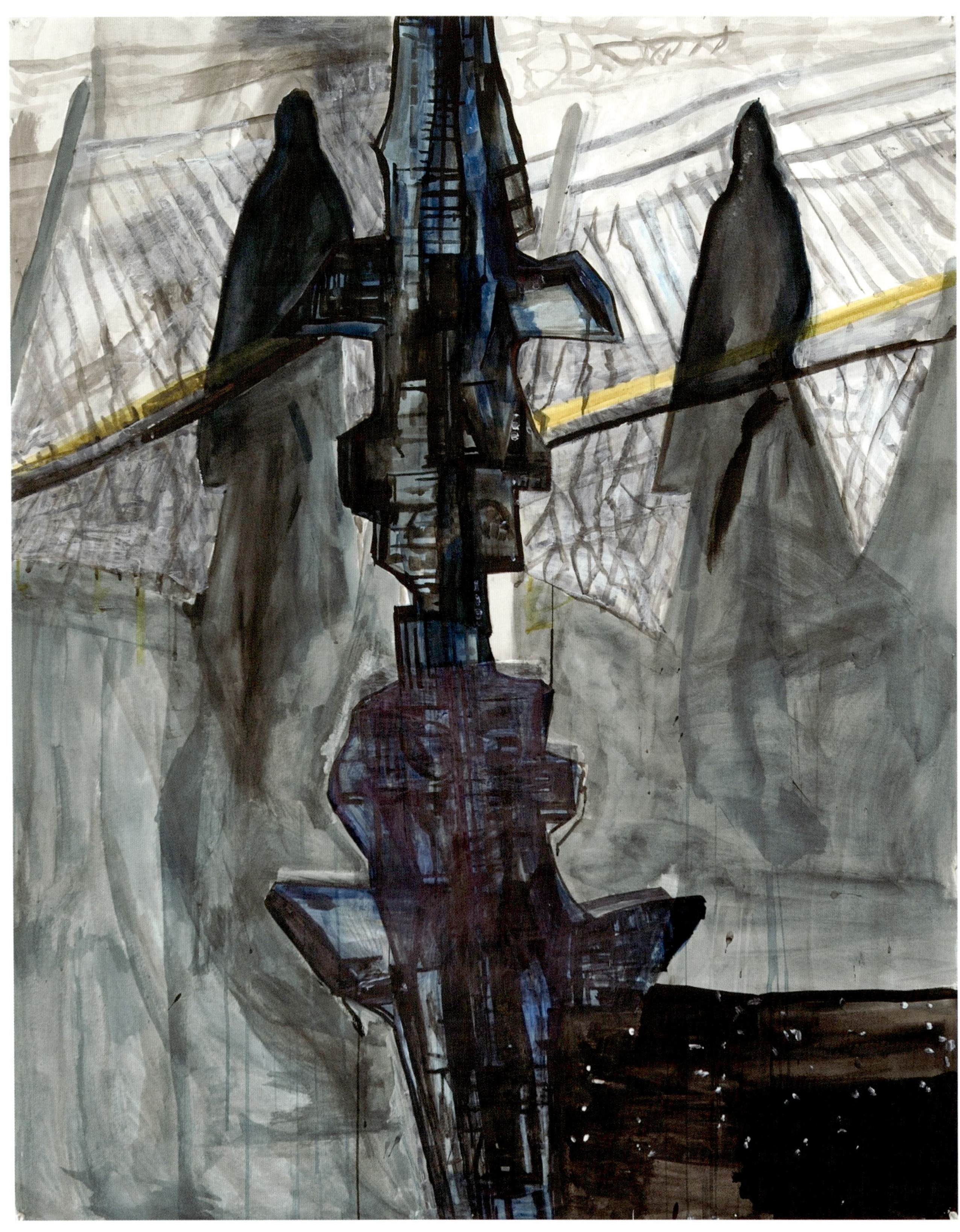

WATCHERS 2016
Ink on paper 150 x 120 cm

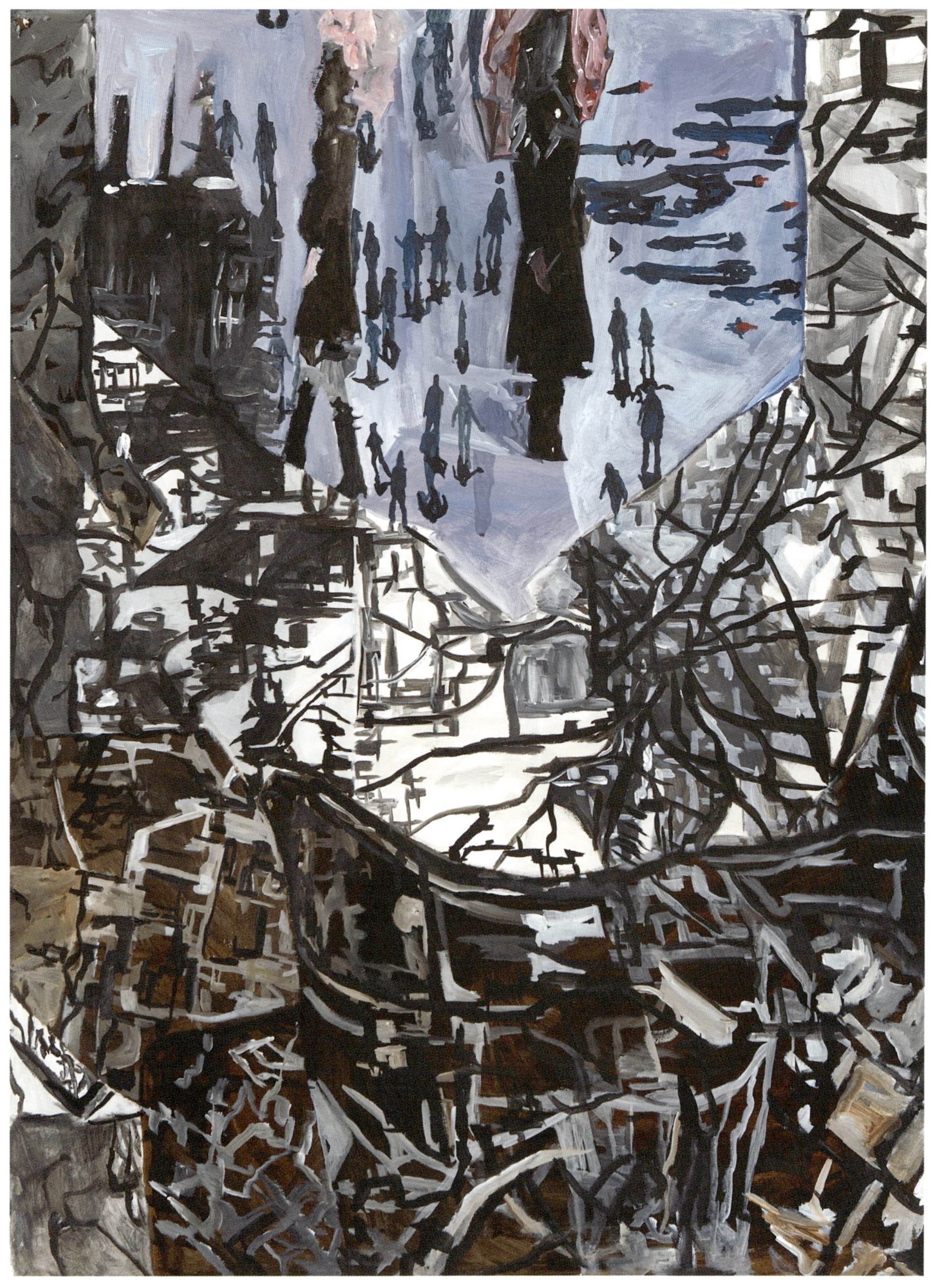

AERIAL SPACE 2016
Acrylic on paper 150 x 120 cm

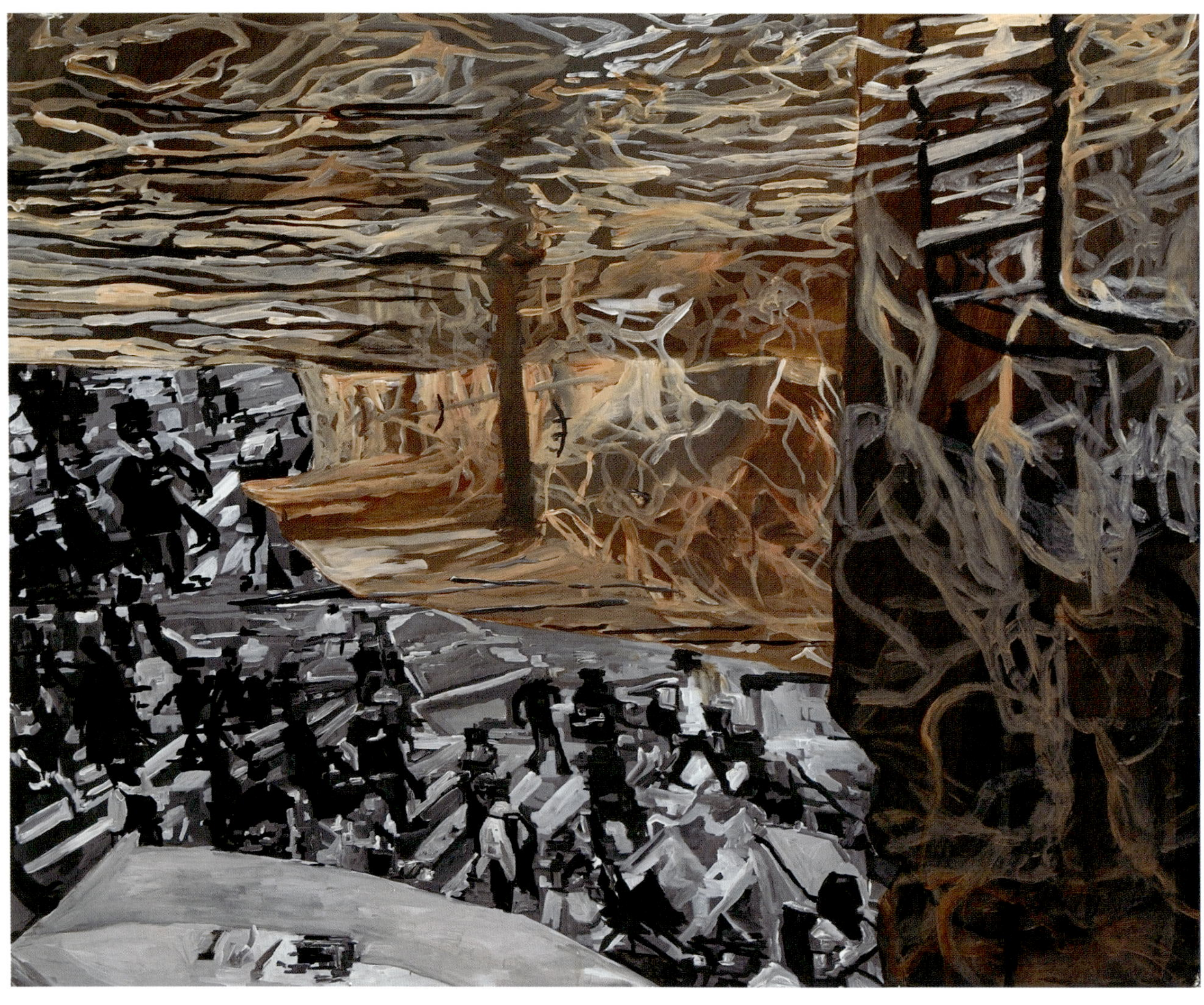

FLOOD 2016
Acrylic on paper 150 x 120 cm

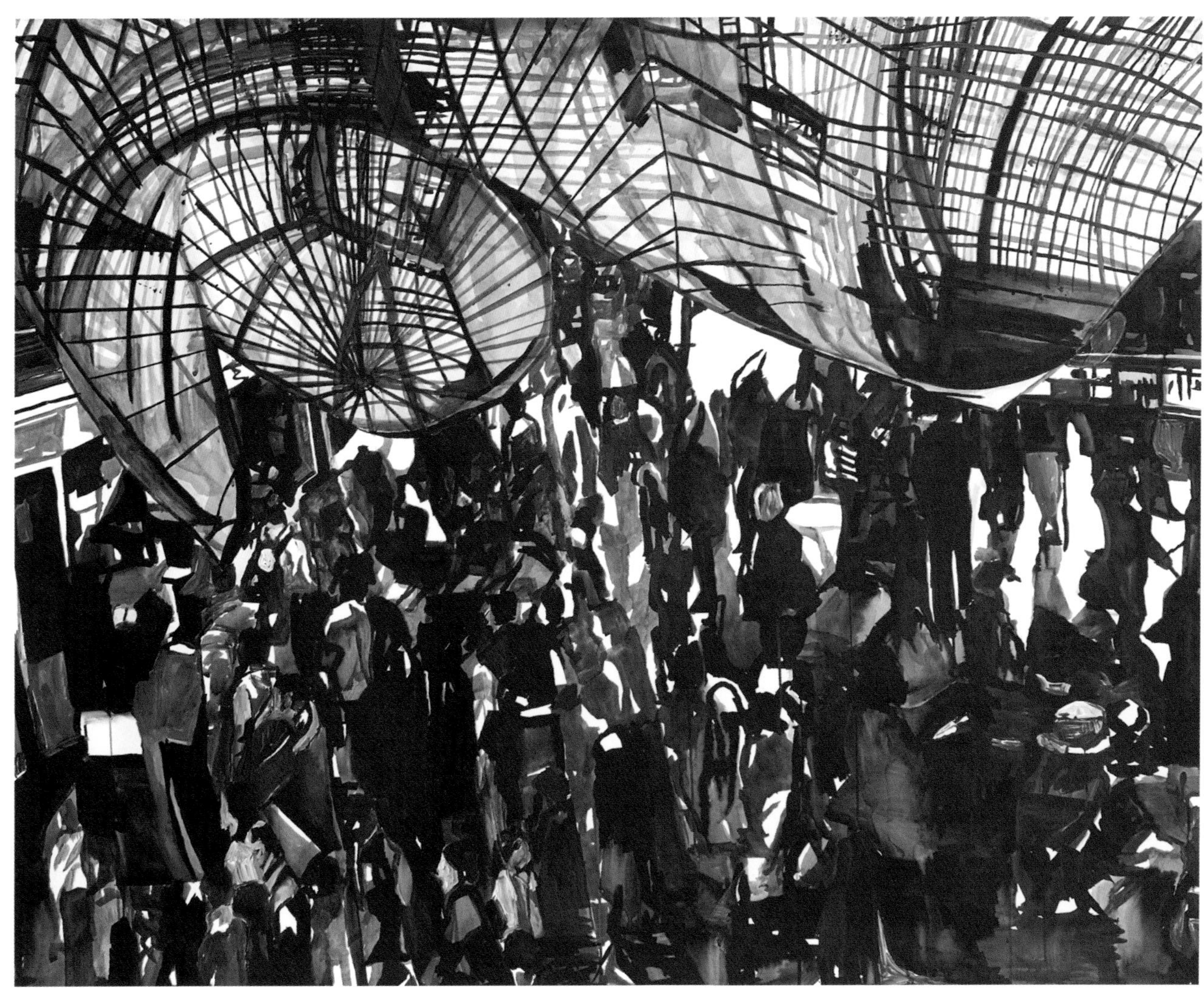

STEEL WEBS 2016
Ink on paper 150 x 120 cm

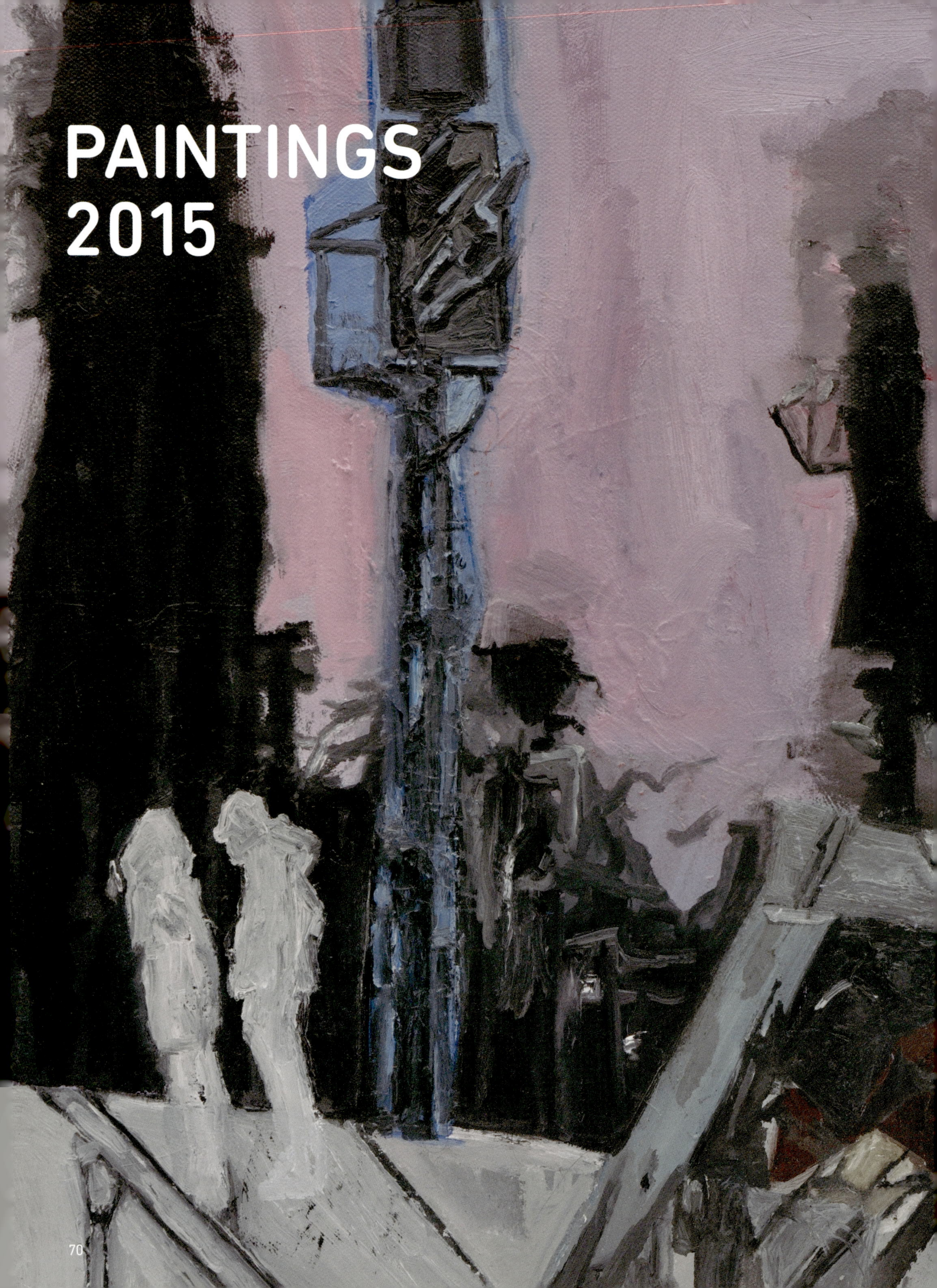
PAINTINGS
2015

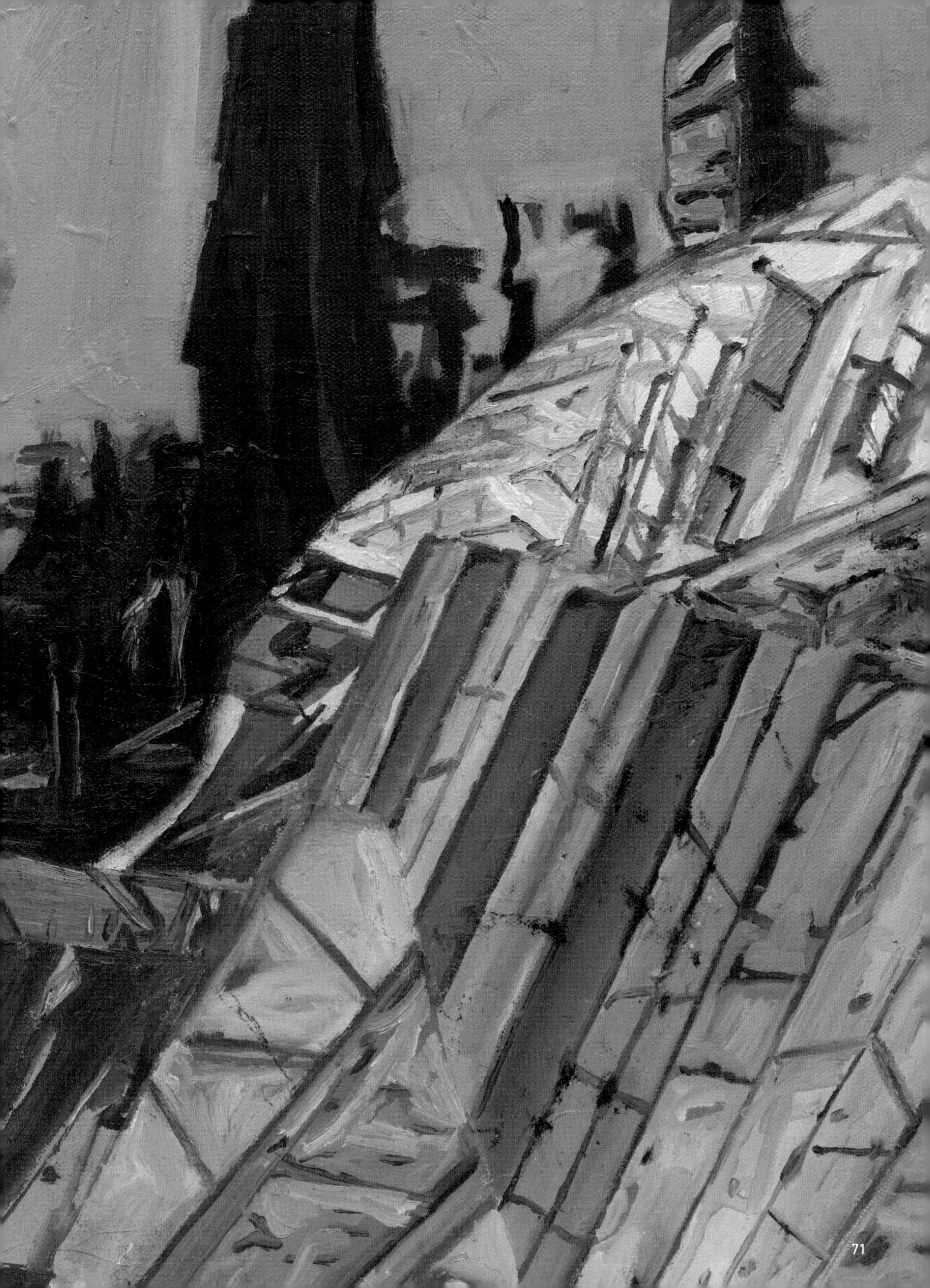

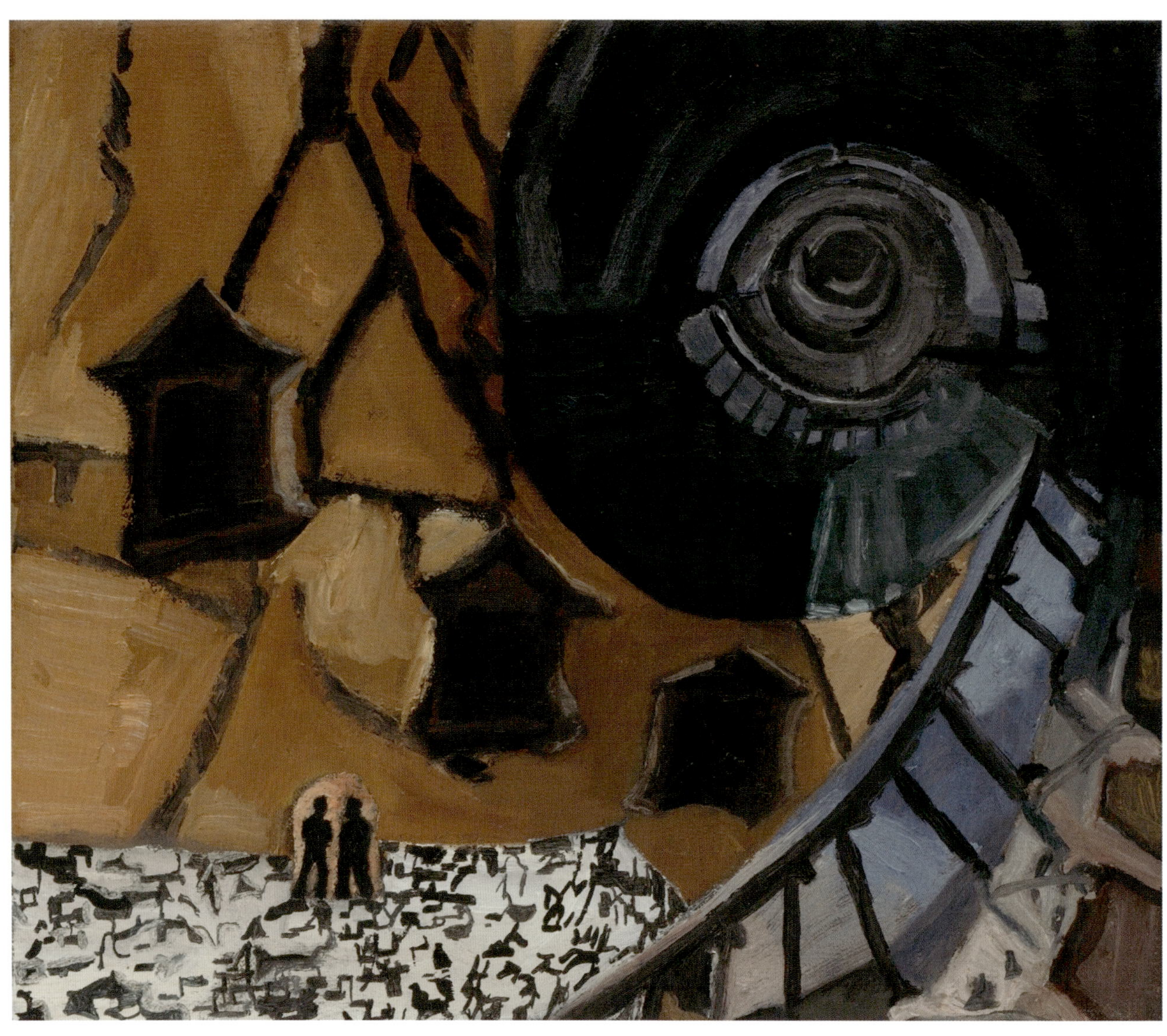

WATCHING 2015
Oil on canvas 30 x 29 cm

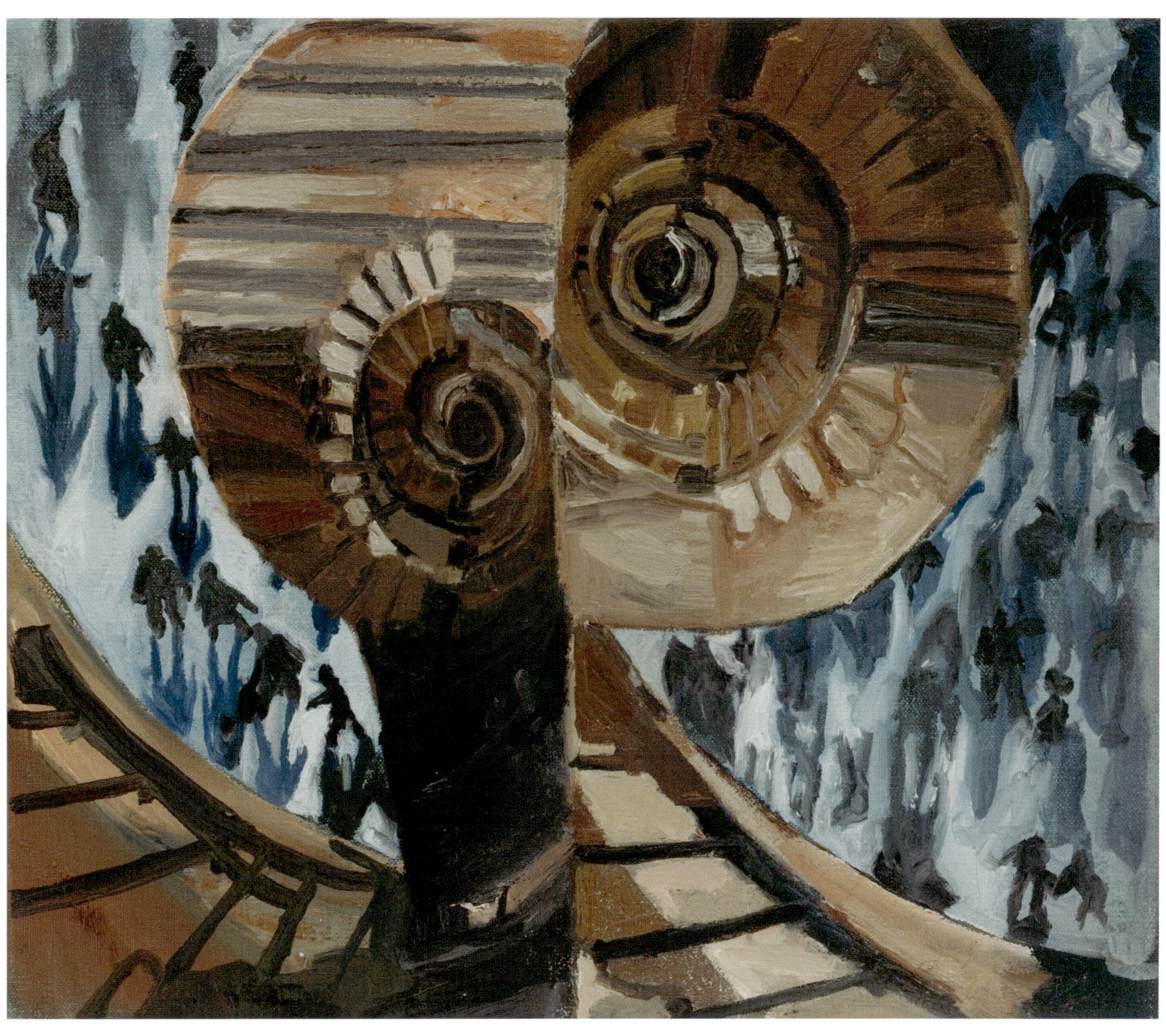

TRANSCENDENCE 2015
Oil on canvas 30 x 29 cm

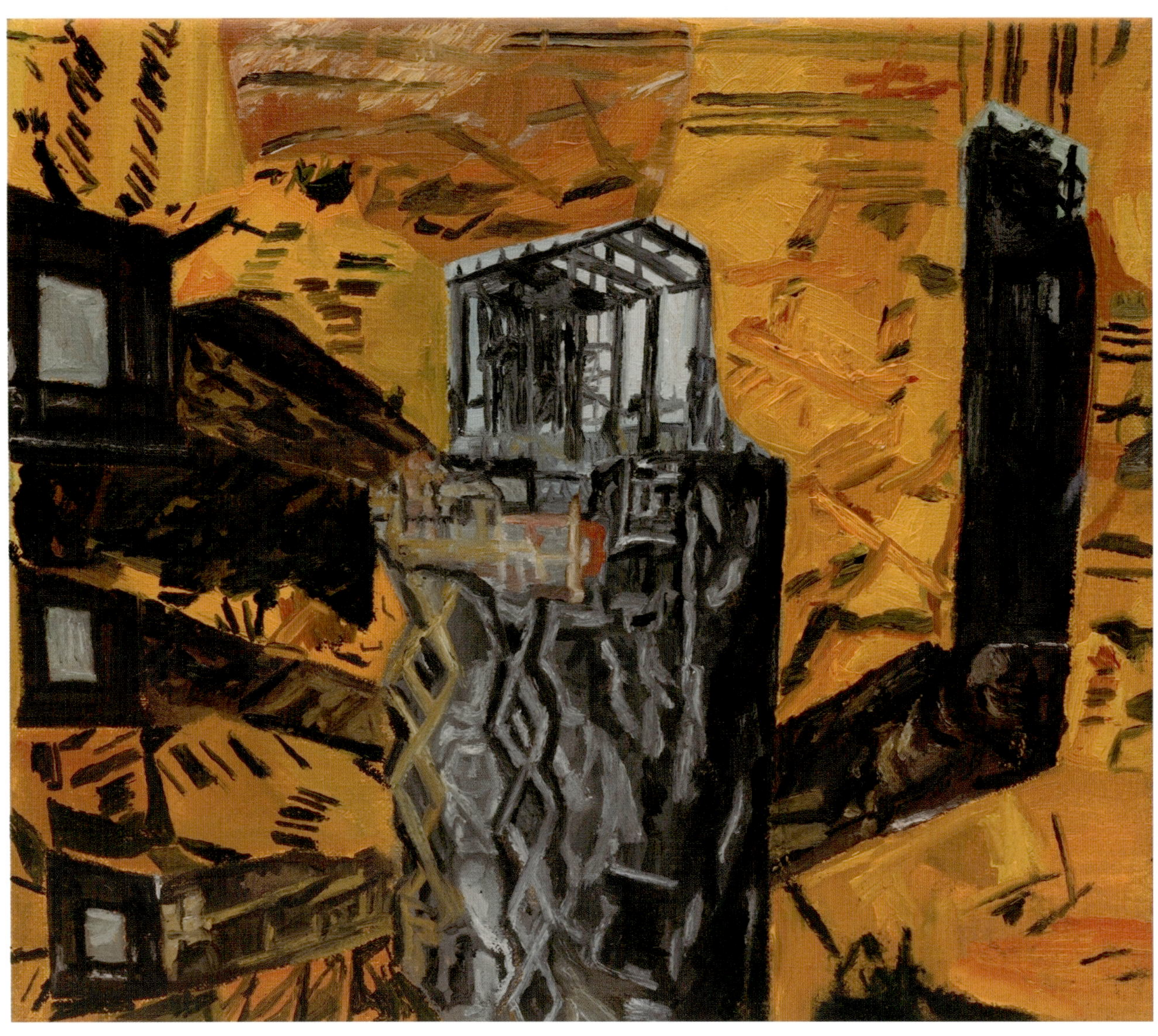

FRAGMENTATION 2015
Oil on canvas 30 x 29 cm

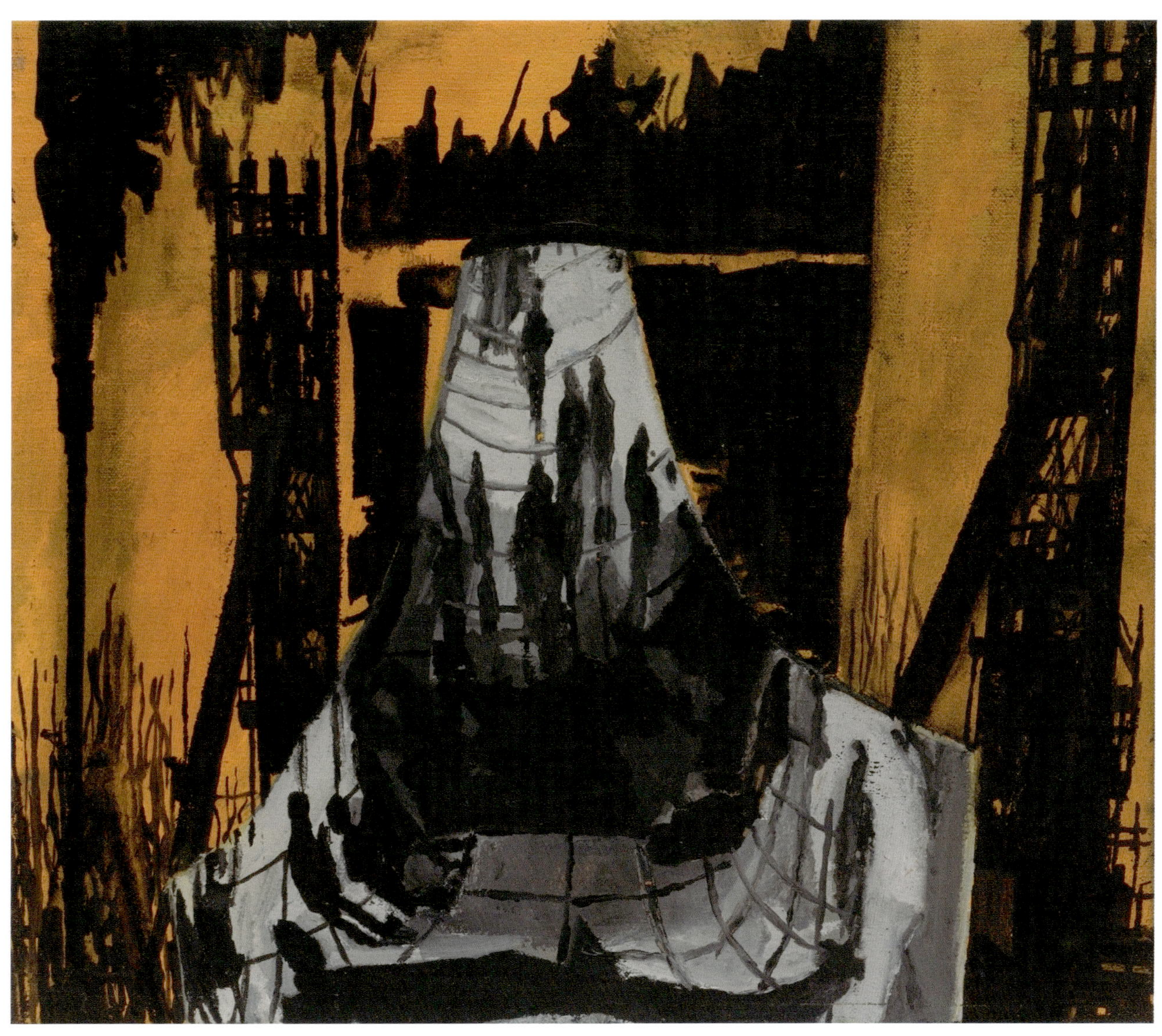

VESSEL 2015
Oil on canvas 30 x 29 cm

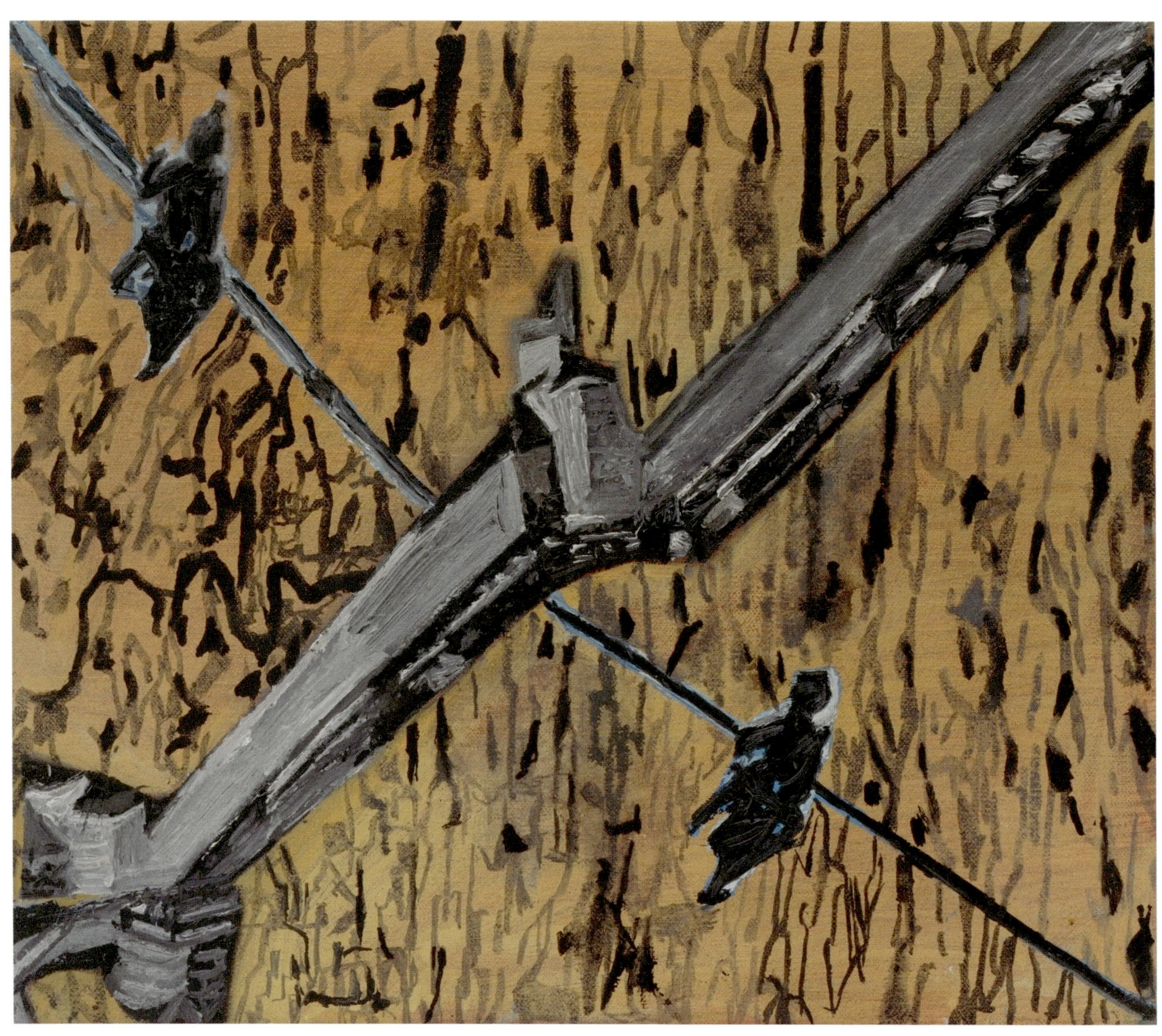

FLOATING 2015
Oil on canvas 30 x 29 cm

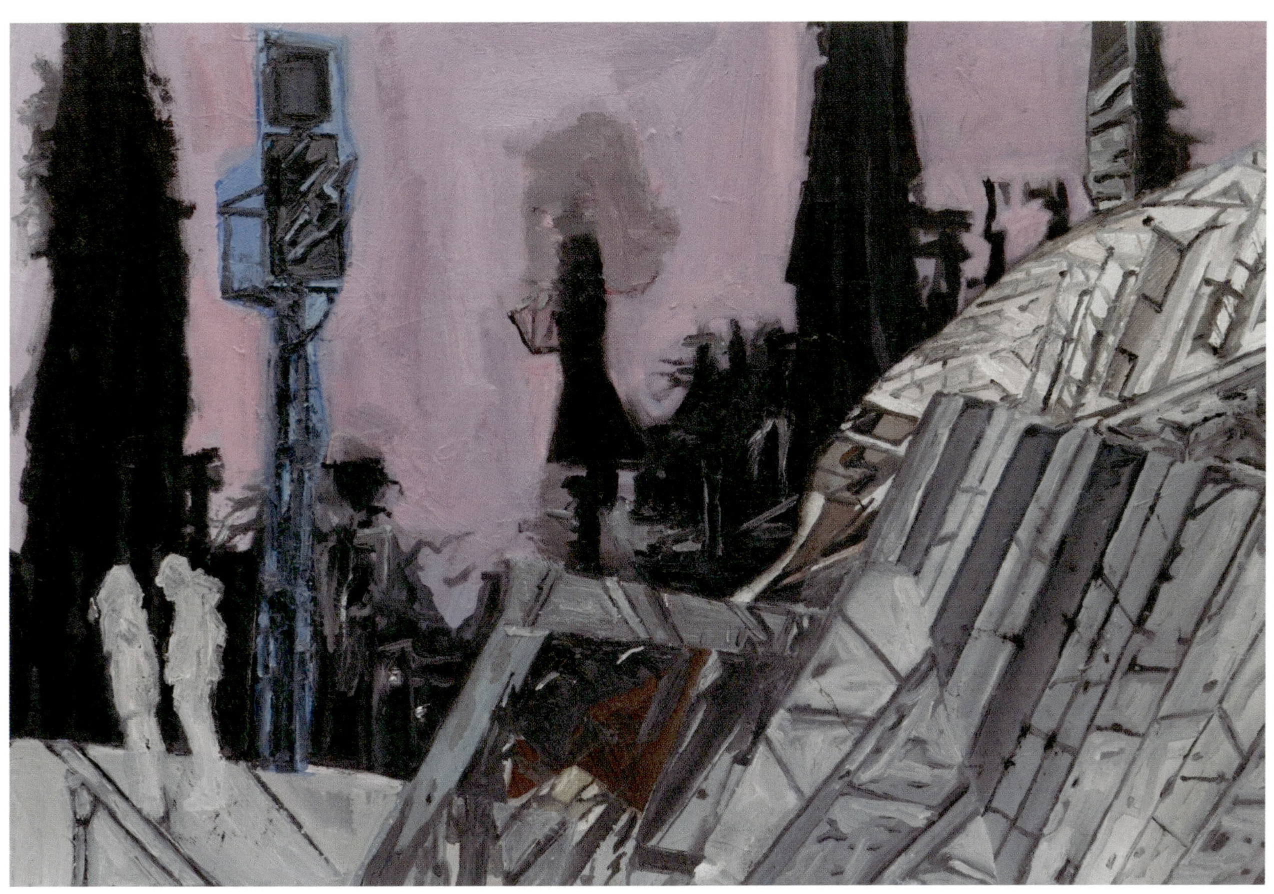

RUIN 2015
Oil on canvas 42 x 30 cm

CONTRIBUTORS

DR AMANDA DRAPER has worked as museum professional for twenty years and has been Curator of Art and Exhibitions at the Victoria Gallery and Museum, University of Liverpool since January 2018. Her PhD addresses representations of gender in Victorian visual culture but her interest in Western art spans from the 1660s to contemporary. As an exhibition curator Amanda strives to engage as wide an audience as possible in the enjoyment and understanding of art.

DR LAUREN ELKIN is the author of *Flaneuse Women Walk the City*. She lives in Paris and Liverpool.

DR GRAEME GILLOCH is Reader in Sociology at Lancaster University. The author of three books on the German Critical Theorists Walter Benjamin and Siegfried Kracauer and co-author of a study of the contemporary Turkish film director Nuri Bilge Ceylan, his work focuses on the relationship between cultural critique, visual culture (especially film) and urban experience and memory. He has published numerous articles and essays on cultural theorists such as Jean Baudrillard and Marc Augé, and writers such as W. G. Sebald, Paul Auster, Orhan Pamuk, China Miéville and Alain Mabanckou. He is currently an international research consultant for two projects: one on film, montage and the city at Pusan National University, South Korea, and the other on fragmentation, reconfiguration and urbanism at the Universidade Nova, Lisboa, Portugal.

Graeme is the co-curator with Michael Hall of *Invisible Print Studio* (London) for the *The Arca Project* exhibition (2017, 2018) and a new series of photographic works *A–Z (Anderswo – Zentralpark)*.

JAI CHUHAN (Jagjit Chuhan) is an Indian born British artist who studied at UCL Slade School of Fine Art. Her paintings have been exhibited internationally including in Italy, Sweden, Belgium, China, Singapore and in the UK including at Tate Liverpool; Barbican, London; Ikon, Birmingham; Arnolfini, Bristol; Watermans Arts Centre, London; Commonwealth Institute, London; Horizon Gallery (Indian Arts Council in the UK), London; recently in Liverpool Biennial 2014; Asia Triennial Manchester 2011 and 2014, Bluecoat, Liverpool 2017, HOME, Manchester 2018. Her paintings are in collections including Arts Council Collection; University of Liverpool Art Collection; Cartwright Hall, Bradford; Grosvenor Museum, Chester; Usher Gallery, Lincoln; Tate Archive. She is Professor of International Art at Liverpool John Moores University.

JASMIR CREED is an artist based in Manchester and London.
She studied at Wimbledon College of Art, University of the Arts
London. She has been artist in residence at Paper Gallery,
Manchester and Castlefield Gallery Manchester New Art Spaces
in 2016. Recent exhibitions include *Urban Forest*, a solo exhibition
at Delta House Studios, London 2017; *Lynn Painter Stainers Prize*,
Mall Galleries, London 2017; *CGP Open*, London 2016; *We all Draw*
at the Bargehouse Oxo Tower, London 2015 curated by Tania
Kovats and Kelly Chorpening, *Interim* at The Crypt Gallery,
London 2014. Her work with Tate Collective on *Who are you?* was
shown at Tate Liverpool 2016, and a painting commissioned by
Imperial War Museum North in 2017 is on permanent display.

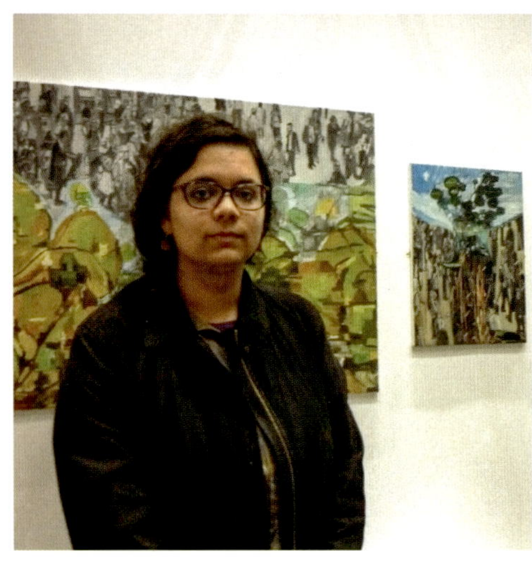